Cognitive Faith

Science, Religion, God and You

By Sue Sorensen

Publishing

© 2018 by Sue Sorensen
All rights reserved. No part of this publication may be reproduced, distributed, or transmitted in any form or by any means, including photocopying, recording, or other electronic or mechanical methods, without the prior written permission of the publisher, except in the case of brief quotations embodied in critical reviews and certain other noncommercial uses permitted by copyright law.

For permission requests, write to the publisher,
"Attention: Permissions Coordinator."

What Really Matters® Publishing
827 N Hollywood Way #522
Burbank, CA 91505
www.wrmpublishing.com
mail@wrmpublishing.com

ISBN: 978 0 9842187 8 3   Paperback Print Edition
ISBN: 978 0 9842187 5 2   E-Book Edition

Introduction

Who is allowed to write a book about faith? Is faith the exclusive realm of pastors, missionaries, religious leaders, or perhaps a celebrity or other notable scholar? I am none of these things. I cannot know if many people will care about or share my view of faith, but I do hope that some will.

While my faith has been long in formation, *Cognitive Faith*, the book, had a more recent genesis. As an avid reader, I select books from a wide range of topics. I enjoy exploring new subjects and new takes on familiar ones. In that spirit and because it was on a recommended reading list, I read *Lies We Believe about God* by William Paul Young. (Atria Books, re-print, 2018) I found the title interesting and knew nothing about Young's previous books. But, with its provocative title, I was interested to see what this

Cognitive Faith

projected best-seller offered. The book was a thoughtful exploration of Young's interpretation of and challenges to traditional Christian tenets, which got me thinking about my own take on Christianity.

Raised as a lightweight Protestant in a middle-class Southern California suburb, I was not force-fed religion. The churches I attended over the years were generally Presbyterian or non-denominational and presented a regime of Jesus-loves-you-and-all-the-little-children, Bible-light, do-good lessons. As a child I was drawn to the church and its positive messages. Even as I later abandoned church-going, I believed for many years, and still do to some extent, that I had received from those early, easy-going church experiences a solid moral foundation for my life.

In my late elementary school years, I found I had a thirst for learning. As a family, we were fortunate enough to have three sets of encyclopedias in the house, certainly not through financial capability, but because my dad was for a short time an encyclopedia salesman. I loved poring over those glossy books, randomly reading about topics. One set was simply called *Science*. I can remember holding one of the heavy, baby-blue volumes with its vibrant color photo inset on the cover, and reading about photosynthesis, gravity, and the universe. I did well in school, went on to college and collected a few degrees, and eventually went on to have a fulfilling career in business.

Introduction

When did religious faith fall away? There was not an exact time or place or issue that I can point to that challenged and ruined religion for me. Instead, I admit that over time religion just seemed more and more archaic to me. In school and through my own passion for knowledge, I was learning other things, *fact-based* things. With growing maturity and intellect, I found myself dismissing, point by point, the ideas of my childhood religion and religion in general.

Christianity and the Bible presented highly unlikely explanations of the world and of ancient events, the most fantastical tale being that the world and all creatures and lands were created in six days. Old Testament aside, the whole Jesus story was riddled with non-starters, including Immaculate Conception, being the literal and only son of God and the one and only path to salvation, raising the dead, walking on water, and resurrection from the dead, just to name a few. Christianity did not present these stories as allegories but asked me, unapologetically, to take them literally.

Furthermore, the simple do-right, do-good principles that I had understood and embraced as a child were, I found, only part of a bigger set of religious doctrines, which, as I grew older, gave me other concerns. I was surprised by the shift in tone when I transitioned from mostly positive children's Sunday School to adult Sunday services. Already sensitive to the unlikely truth of Biblical stories, I listened to the sermons and the rhetoric, and, even

Cognitive Faith

at a young age, found many of the doctrines to be manipulative: for example, having to accept and declare, repeatedly, that Jesus is one's Savior. Pejorative: for example, saying we are risking hell, damnation, and the wrath of God if we fail to abide by the church's tenets. And, occasionally contradictory: for example, attending church faithfully was presented as important, but the Bible says that praying in church offers no reward in heaven (Matthew 6:5-8). Plus, there was my continuing and growing issue with the many fictions presented. The Protestant world I had supposed to be simple, loving, and tolerant, had, I realized, complicated beliefs that could be quite judgmental and rigid.

By middle school, religious zeal began to frighten me. I saw that Christianity and other organized religions sometimes condemned and judged, spawning hate and divisiveness. When I was about eleven years old, I remember being shocked speechless when a woman in a church activity room where I was attending a craft-filled summer Bible school pointed to a small, dime-store Celtic cross I was wearing on a chain. She asked me if I understood that the cross was a symbol and then said Protestants do not worship symbols. "Those filthy Papists," she hissed, "worship crosses and saints, and kiss the damned rings." She righteously asserted that *we* worship only Jesus and God. Later I had to ask my mother what a "Papist" was, and it was my first experience with religious hate. Even at that tender age, I felt that there was something very wrong with a church whose God supposedly loved all the little children of the world on one hand but decried those filthy Papists on the other.

In my mid-teens through my twenties, I drifted toward agnosticism. During those years, I was living an extremely rowdy lifestyle, and religion and faith seemed at odds with my sketchy, hard-partying behavior. Then, in my late twenties, emerging from what might politely be called a raucous early adulthood, I got sober. No need to chronicle here the ups and downs of my drug and alcohol-addled years, but as some readers may know, recovery in a 12-Step program is based on turning your will and your life over to a higher power or God. Humm. Okay. For me, a new faith was required.

I was asked by an early reader of this manuscript to explain more fully the faith *requirement* for 12-Step recovery. The reader, not particularly familiar with 12-Step programs, pointed out, rightly, that I stated without much explanation that my exploration, or re-exploration, of faith was initially motivated by my desire to sustain sobriety, which was true. He suggested that, if indeed the 12-Step program was so inextricably related to the eventual emergence of Cognitive Faith, a more substantial explanation was warranted. I was, however, resistant to delving too deeply into my story and "the program," as we call it. I did not, and still do not want to have *Cognitive Faith* be a book pigeon-holed as only for or about drug or alcohol dependency or 12-Step recovery.

Cognitive Faith

Still, I was eventually convinced of the importance of sharing a bit more in this introduction about how and why getting and being sober through 12-Step programs compelled my personal faith journey. I believe, though, and want to stress that *many* people search for and explore faith without being drug addicts or alcoholics.

All 12-Step recovery programs are based on—no surprise—twelve steps. Alcoholic Anonymous was the first 12-Step program and is the most familiar. Many other 12-Step programs exist, though, focusing on various substances or compulsion issues. I personally spent much of my early recovery in Cocaine Anonymous. With minor wording variations, all 12-Step programs outline the same recovery process. Of the twelve steps, six specifically mention God or a higher power. Step one simply asserts that we admitted to being powerless over our substance use and that our lives had become unmanageable. Then the second step states, "we came to believe that a power greater than ourselves could restore us to sanity." And, in step three, we turn our will and our life over to the care of God, as we understand God. I will not review every step, but these first steps are known as the foundation steps and are very clearly based in faith.

You might ask, why did I pursue 12-Step program recovery if I was, as stated, agnostic and living a religion- and faith-free life at that time? Why not go to a treatment center or try some form of therapy? I can only say that I was at a low point when I sought help. In fact, few people

Introduction

merrily decide to get clean and sober when their lives are working well. I was employed, but marginally, as a waitress, despite my college degrees. I was drinking up to a quart of hard liquor daily and smoking rock cocaine often, using my nightly cash tips to finance my carousing. I regularly found myself in compromising situations and was having blackouts. Not surprisingly, my personal and emotional life was a mess. I had no money to speak of. I barely afforded my $350 a month rent – even with an alcoholic boyfriend living with me. I had no insurance. I had no caring family members offering to help or even involved in my life at that time.

Attending a 12-Step program is free. There is no membership requirement or commitment. Frankly, I had no idea what I was hoping for when I initially reached that emotional bottom that drove me to seek help, other than wanting a reprieve from my current unhappiness. I did not particularly envision long-term sobriety. I just felt, in a hopeless and impenetrable way, that I could not continue as I was. Therapy or a hospital stay did not even occur to me as a realistic possibility. Perhaps if I had been injured in a car accident or arrested – entirely possible events at that time – I might have been pressed by authorities toward another path for recovery. Instead, I embarked on sobriety by calling a hotline and being directed to attend a 12-Step meeting.

I did not like the God stuff I heard being discussed in the meetings and read about in the 12-Step literature. But I found myself setting aside my opinions about God and faith

Cognitive Faith

in the earliest days of my sobriety. I was told I could consider meetings a higher power and think more about God later, once I had some days clean and sober. Remarkably, I did stay clean and sober. For the first time in a dozen years, I strung together a growing number of consecutive days free from all drugs and alcohol. It was at that juncture that I started to feel hope: hope that I might have a different life. It was also at that point when I suspected that, to maintain the hoped-for recovery, avoiding the God thing would not work long-term.

Of course, I did not immediately and easily transition to Cognitive Faith. First, I struggled with years of uncomfortable and inelegant attempts to adapt the Protestant religion and God as I knew God in my early life, into a viable "higher power" to underpin my sobriety. That semblance of faith worked well enough to keep me sober for a few years. But after those first few years I once again began to struggle with the tenets of religion. Furthermore, as often happens in sobriety, symptoms of my underlying dis-ease—for me, feelings of personal inadequacy and social alienation —were resurfacing. With the bad feelings came unhealthy, self-sabotaging behaviors: for example, taking a second job as a cocktail waitress in a nightclub at one point and dating a drug dealer at another. The first couple of years were indeed tenuous for me.

I was in a faith dilemma. I suspected that, if I could not sort out the God and faith thing, I might stray from recovery. It was certainly clear that whatever faith I had

Introduction

was not a cornerstone of internal strength and fortification for me. When I read William Paul Young's book recently, I admired his willingness to challenge some of the basic tenets of his Christian beliefs. But I also reflected on how I, back in the early years of my sobriety, struggled while trying to spin Christianity, through great machinations, into a viable faith to support my recovery. I know I am not alone in this struggle. Even some progressive religious proponents, like Young, seem to be looking for an interpretation that can make Christianity make sense.

Within a couple of years, I just accepted that Christianity did not work for me. On top of my inability to manipulate Christianity sufficiently to be useful, I had no attraction to *any* of the various other spiritual ideologies or programs I was exposed to over the years.

In the seventies and eighties, when I was a teen and through my twenties, lots of out-of-the-box spiritual or religious ideologies were popularized. My own mother attended an EST session. Hare Krishna parades occurred, and recruiters opined daily along the Venice Beach boardwalk, where I often lazed off my hang-overs. Transcendental Meditation was practiced by a few of my older friends. I even read L. Ron Hubbard's book *Scientology*. Most of these "religions" or spiritual movements were presented without many of the trappings of traditional religious rhetoric, but devotees were still off-puttingly zealous. I was not drawn to any of these ideologies.

Cognitive Faith

Over the subsequent years, some of these spiritual movements were tainted by cult or fad status. In fact, most of the pseudo-religions popularized in my youth did not endure. Some truly were cults, and dangerously so. I think here most prominently of Jim Jones's People's Temple and the Moonies of the Unification Church, but there were others, less nefarious but still debunked. Regarding Scientology, years later I read with disappointment the accounts of the inner workings of that so-called religion in the tell-all *Troublemaker* by Leah Remini and *Going Clear* by Lawrence Wright.

So, for me in the nineties, though sober, my faith in terms of Christianity was clearly shaky. In casting about for spiritual grounding, though, I felt no attraction for pop religions, non-Christian religions, quasi-religious sects, or new-age spiritual groups. For a time, as you will read later, I adopted a Star Wars philosophy of faith, but this whimsical variety of spirituality did little to alleviate the troubling unease I felt. I was concerned, and rightly, over the resurfacing of unhealthy behaviors, and I had seen, over the years, countless recovering friends return to drinking and using drugs. A few actually died, a few went to jail, a few returned to recovery, albeit diminished in circumstances, and some just stayed away, once again living the unhappy life of practicing alcoholics or addicts.

For me, looking back on it now, it was clear I had reached a point where I needed a stronger, more viable faith. I conceded that Christianity could not be the basis for

Introduction

my spirituality. I needed a practical, serious faith that spoke to and satisfied my mind.

Eventually, I found myself writing about and defining my own ideas about faith and God. As I wrote, I ascribed to my personal brand of faith a set of premises chronicled in the following chapters. Embracing this faith, which I began to refer to as Cognitive Faith, my life and circumstances significantly improved. But a fair question is: why would I choose to share my ideas about faith? The answer is simply that I believe there are others in the world that might embrace Cognitive Faith. I believe there are people looking for a path to some form of spirituality that makes sense, that does not condemn or tear others down, that can empower and buoy the soul, and that does not require disengaging the mind. I believe there are many people like me who struggle with religion but can or might benefit from faith.

I was asked by another early reader if *Cognitive Faith*, the book, is geared primarily toward troubled people or people with emotional or substance abuse problems. The short answer is no. However, when I reviewed the early manuscript, with my expanded discussion of 12-Step program experience, I saw that many of the examples I used, and of course my own life anecdotes might, indeed, lead some to wonder if Cognitive Faith applies only to broken people. So here let me say that I can categorize potential readers into a number of groups.

Cognitive Faith

First are the happy, healthy seekers. I think people with open minds and general interest in matters of faith might read and consider the propositions of *Cognitive Faith* with interest. They may or may not subscribe to a conventional religious faith, actively or at some point in their past, but, regardless of their current level of spirituality, may adopt or take away some insights or points of agreement from *Cognitive Faith*. I include in this group agnostic and atheist readers that may or may not be swayed by the concepts. I very much like to include the agnostic and atheist population, as I feel a kinship with these skeptics, so long as they are willing to engage with and consider the hows and whys of their beliefs.

Another group of readers might be those devout in an orthodox religion. While *Cognitive Faith* certainly challenges some tenets of traditional religion, I want to stress that you *can* adopt Cognitive Faith *and* maintain your association with a traditional religion. The human brain is perfectly capable of managing and even embracing doctrines that conflict. My intention in sharing my concerns about Christianity and other organized religions was to illustrate why conventional religion did not work for me and why it offends the sensibilities of many others. Still, I sincerely hope that *Cognitive Faith* might encourage the religiously devout to explore some of the intellectual and social challenges that maintaining traditional religious beliefs may engender.

Introduction

Finally, there is a group of potential readers who, like me, have faced large or small personal issues, substance abuse issues or other dysfunctions. They may or may not subscribe to a traditional religious faith, or may be agnostic or atheist, but are exploring *Cognitive Faith* as a possible source of an empowering faith that might help them overcome their challenges.

While writing *Cognitive Faith*, I did do a bit of research on some of the concepts of faith or science explored in this book. I also extracted thoughts or points from a wide assortment of other general reading I have done over the years on topics such as philosophy, psychology, anthropology, biology, physics, and history. The research and reading material have helped shape, support, and articulate concepts, but this book is not a thesis, nor a research book, and the annotations should not be considered exhaustive. Readers are encouraged to explore the topics and arguments presented. In fact, Cognitive Faith has at its core a desire to allow and encourage rational thought and exploration of truth, certainly not to be the final word on it.

My hope is that *Cognitive Faith* may address questions and feelings that many people in our world struggle with regarding religion and faith. I sincerely hope it will stimulate reflection on faith and suspect it will challenge people's thinking. And, my final hope is that *Cognitive Faith* will provide a path to and allowance for faith even if you are a devout realist, allowing any reader to integrate faith into modern-day, life-enhancing action.

Part One
Science

The Big Bang and Evolutionary Science

Bang! Actually, make that a big bang! In fact, a really BIG BANG! That's the start of the universe. Now you might be wondering what this has to do with faith. You may be thinking that the Big Bang as a topic is unassociated with faith, since Christianity and other religious creeds do not generally integrate the Big Bang theory into their explanations of our world's origin. I have a problem with that. Science can very credibly demonstrate that the universe is expanding from a dense center and becomes sparser at the outer edges, supporting the Big Bang singularity theory. That theory puts the universe at about thirteen or fourteen billion years old. Astrophysics, astronomy, and mathematics support the theory. I am not an astrophysicist, but I do not have to be to accept this science. The proof is compelling. I can grasp the scientific explanation that rationally convinces me that the universe is vast, expanding, and started a very long time ago (with an allowance of plus or minus a few billion years).

Much later came the earth and biological life. Current estimates put the earth's formation at somewhere between four and six billion years ago. With just a marginal understanding of solar systems and how they form, I am convinced of earth's ancient provenance as explained by science. Next came life. About a billion years after the earth formed, single-celled life emerged, followed over the next few billion years by more and more complex forms of life. At about 250 million years ago, the age of reptiles and our beloved dinosaurs began, followed by the emergence of the prehistoric mammals at about 150 million years ago. According to scientific evidence, the ascent of primates began with the earliest primates 65 million years ago. Then starting about five or six million years ago, a progression of near-human species appeared, along with early versions of many other modern mammal species. Homo sapiens came into existence about one million years ago, and by about eleven thousand years ago, these modern humans were the only remaining humanoids left on the planet.

All the above statements are scientifically substantiated, though I allow for the possibility of some future timeline adjustments as we are better able to date the past. Still, there is evidence. The geological, fossil, and archeological evidence is undeniable. Yet, at this point, I may have lost a good many Christian and other religious readers.

Which takes me back to the question of faith. The Oxford English Dictionary defines faith as a noun, meaning, "1) complete trust or confidence in someone or something," and "2) strong belief in the doctrines of a religion, based on spiritual conviction rather than proof." Religion, especially Christianity, relies heavily on the second definition. I rely more heavily on the first.

I began to struggle at an early age with conventional religion, because I found many of the propositions of Christianity questionable. I had difficulty trusting and having confidence in my faith, because Christianity put forth explanations of the world's origins and ancient events that seemed implausible. Though contrary evidence exists, I was asked by religious pundits to nevertheless accept, in faith, the religious version of truth. As a result, even as a youngster I questioned a faith that asked congregants to disbelieve common truths.

"Jane," a friend of mine, related the following story. "I had just moved across the country for my job. I was in a new state without any family and in a new plant where I knew no one. So, I began testing out co-workers to find a potential lunch buddy."

Cognitive Faith

"I would always start with chatting about routine work stuff. If I felt the co-worker was nice," she said, "I would suggest that maybe we could have lunch together sometime."

"One lady from the accounting team was bubbly, friendly, and about my age," Jane continued, "When I suggested we grab lunch together some time, she readily agreed. A few days later we walked over to a nearby diner. After we ordered our lunch I made some innocuous comment about a dinosaur exhibit I had visited over the past weekend at a local museum."

"This woman's face transformed," Jane said. "She looked me dead in the eye and coldly stated that the museum was full of blasphemy. She told me dinosaurs are not real, and the world is only about 6,000 years old." Jane was surprised to realize that she had moved into a part of the country where Christian literalists were not uncommon.

"I was stunned." She went on, "Worse, we still had the remainder of lunchtime ahead of us. You know, where do you go from there? I instantly knew we were not going to have a rational discussion of this. I just smiled, mumbled something to the effect of 'alright,' trying very hard to not have any sarcasm or tone of disbelief, and then changed the subject to talk about the plant. But really, wow. All I could think was, wow, these people actually exist."

William of Occam, a Franciscan friar from the 14th century, postulated that, when determining the correct answer for an evidentiary question, the simplest answer, that is, the answer that successfully accounts for all the facts or evidence with the fewest layers of explanation, or adjustments of facts, is generally the best answer. Occam's razor, as this philosophical principle is called, suggests that given two solutions, the solution that requires the least manipulation of the facts is preferred. Of course, first the solution must account for all the facts. (see Fig. 1)

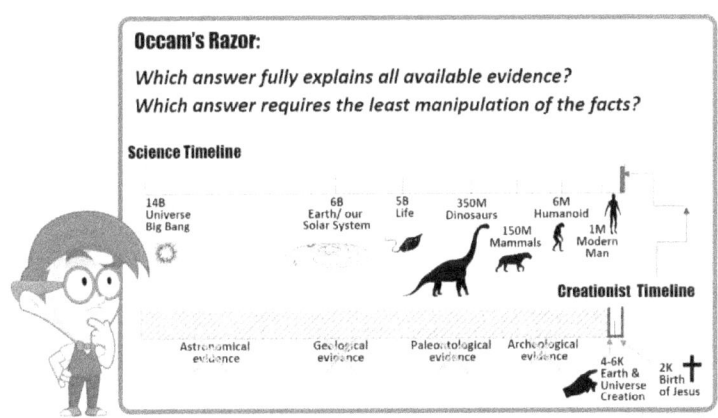

Fig. 1

So, if the question is, for example, how old is the world? or the universe? any answer must take into account the facts of fossils, other geological evidence, and astronomical data. If a faith asks you to believe their propositions, their answers *should align with* what we know to be true. "...therefore, where we have clear evidence... reason is the proper judge; and revelation...cannot in such cases invalidate its decrees: nor can we be obliged, where we have the clear and evident sentience of reason, to quit it for the contrary opinion, under a pretense that it is matter of faith: which can have no authority against the plain and clear dictates of reason." This was written by John Locke in 1690 in his *Essay Concerning Human Understanding*.

So too with spiritual faith. For me to believe the tenets of a religion, I must feel the propositions being espoused inspire confidence and are trustworthy. In other words, labeling contrary or fantastical propositions "your faith" does not rationally excuse or answer the discrepancies in those propositions versus commonly known facts. My friend and I both found this grown woman's denial of the entire library of geological, paleontological, and archeological evidence, in order to accept and support a religious tenet, disturbing.

Logic and Reasoning

In college, I took a course entitled "Logic and Reasoning" and later developed a corporate course titled Critical Thinking to help managers improve their presentation and assessment of arguments, viewpoints or positions. The content in both cases included an exploration of common reasoning fallacies. (Thank you, Professor Engel.) In presenting an argument or stance, declaring that something is true because it is believed to be true is called circular reasoning. Because the Bible says so or because it is the word of God is not proof. I am sorry to inform ardent believers, but you cannot substantiate a belief with further beliefs. When a person or group presents their belief as "truth," we open the door to the slippery slope of any belief being presented as truth.

In today's world, we do see fantastical propositions presented as fact, quasi-fact, or as profoundly realistic, through movies, television series, and "reality" shows. In the age-old chicken-and-egg dilemma, we cannot know, do people believe these fantasies because our culture, art, literature and other media realistically presents them? Or do we present them because people believe in them? But, yes, according to various polls, people do believe in spontaneous, Biblical-style miracles (71%), angels (80%), ESP and psychic powers (41%), magic and astrology (29%), ghosts (32%), a secret-government, new-world-order conspiracy (28%), spells and witchcraft (19%), zombies and vampires (6% each), and even Bigfoot and unicorns (14% and 6% respectively). To be fair, I suspect that many of the people who present, assert, or simply indulge these beliefs are doing so with tongue in cheek, and I am not too bothered by their harmless avowals. People can believe their own brands of nonsense with little impact to me or my life. People may or may not hold these farfetched beliefs deeply. A belief in zombies, magic, or miracles, is rarely presented in a forum that might challenge or repudiate current scientific knowledge or impact the day-to-day lives of other citizens.

Unexplained Mysteries and Belief in God

But do the substantial number of scientific or reasoning flaws in traditional religious beliefs and rhetoric, preclude any belief in God or spiritual faith? Is faith irreconcilably opposed to science and truth? I will say that some *religions* do staunchly stand apart from scientific knowledge and well-supported facts, as evidenced by so-called Biblical literalists. But does the fact that *most* religions present scientifically flawed beliefs preclude any rational belief or faith in God? To the contrary, despite the wide assortment of dubious or even fantastical explanations of our origins, and assertions of far-fetched early historical events by various human religions, I nevertheless feel that creation is one of the most compelling arguments *for* belief in God or a divine force.

No matter how perfectly we can account for what happened after the Big Bang, a mystery remains, as does the unanswered philosophical question: What *caused* the Big Bang? While matter was being strewn outward, where did "the matter" come from? If the first life on earth sprang into existence a few billion years ago, how did inanimate matter transform into living matter? Science does not have rational answers for these essential questions, and therefore opens the way for a belief that some version of God may yet exist.

Alexander Vilenkin, a cosmologist at Tufts University near Boston, is quoted in an article. "We have very good evidence that there was a Big Bang, so the universe as we know it almost certainly started some 14 billion years ago. But was that the absolute beginning, or was there something before it? It seems like the kind of question that can never be truly answered, because every time someone proposes a solution, someone else can keep asking the annoying question: What happened before *that*?" ("What Came Before the Big Bang?" by Steve Nadis, *Discover Magazine*, Sept 2013)

Fourth-century theologian St. Augustine also wrestled with the question of time and the creation of the universe. And what was his answer? First a disclaimer: St Augustine's question about creation revolved around the *Biblical* interpretation of creation, and still raises some deep controversy, and it must be remembered that he was, after all, a sainted *Christian*. But the interesting and provocative question Augustine raised about God and creation, was "what of the time *before* creation?" His answer? Time itself was part of God's creation, and there simply was no "before." (Mortenson and Galling, *Augustine and the Days of Creation*, January 2012, https://answersingenesis.org/days-of-creation/augustine-on-the-days-of-creation/)

God, that is, an undefinable divine force, as creator of our universe and of life itself, becomes for me a starting place for faith. I found that I could believe in a God, or divine force, that underlies the creation of our universe and the miraculous spark of life, because it allowed me to accept all currently known science, without a requirement that I defy any of the known facts or the timeline as revealed through

[23]

science and scientific evidence. Further, the existence of a God provides an answer to questions as yet unanswered by science, such as how matter came from naught, how life sprung from inanimate material, and indeed how the miraculous complexity and order of life and the world we see all around us came to be. These questions science simply cannot answer.

This leads me briefly to the complicated physics of sub-atomic particles, and in particular, the discovery or confirmation of the Higgs boson in 2012. The Higgs boson has sometimes been referred to in media reports as "the God particle." While I do not claim to have true understanding of sub-atomic physics or bosons, I can grasp some of the high-level explanations as I found in *Smashing Physics* by Jon Butterworth (Headline Books Publishing, 2014). The big hubbub around the Higgs boson is that it seems to provide evidence of a particle with no mass, interacting with other particles, which also initially have no mass, transforming those other particles into particles that have mass. This is why some might see the boson interaction as evidence of a God-like event of creation of matter from naught.

Given this sensationalized "God Particle" interpretation of the Higgs boson discovery, *even if the bosons were indeed the explanation of the "creation" of matter*, you must conclude with Vilenkin's troubling question. "And where did those non-mass particles come from?" I happily embrace whatever we eventually learn. But at present, I still find the origins of the universe and the eventual springing forth of life from it to be miraculous enough to attach my dictionary faith definition, part two, to it: that of spiritual conviction, lacking proof, to which I can without too much concern say I believe "God" did it.

    Albert Einstein, arguably the most eminent scientist in history, was said to have famously and repeatedly been asked to comment on the question of God's existence. Einstein spoke of his early religious beliefs, Jewish beliefs in his case. He claimed to have possessed for a time in his childhood "a deep religiousness," which "came to an abrupt end at the age of twelve." "Through the reading of popular scientific books," he said, "I soon reached the conviction that much in the stories of the Bible could not be true." (*The Cosmic View of Albert Einstein,* edited by Walt Martin and Magna Ott, Sterling Publishing, 2013) Of God, though, and creation, he said, "I see a pattern, but my imagination cannot picture the maker of the pattern. I see the clock, but I cannot envisage the clock-maker." Of faith, which he called religiosity, he said, "My religiosity consists in a humble admiration of the infinitely superior spirit that reveals itself in the little that we, with our weak and transitory understanding, can comprehend of reality."

    I too was enamored in my youth with the church, but later felt compelled to abandon religiosity. But I feel in very good company when I maintain that, even with all available scientific evidence, and despite my disillusionment with religion, like Einstein, I feel the world nevertheless offers enough mystery and awe to support faith in a divine power, which I believe created this universe, and which I choose to call God.

Laws of Physics – Indestructability

Though I am a corporate educator by trade, and a lay person as far as science is concerned, I am nevertheless a life-long lover of science. Still, as already mentioned, I have no trouble attributing the origins of the universe to a divine power that I call God. Beyond creation, however, I cannot help but see divinity in the elegant laws of science and the intricate workings of the world. Workings set into place and played out over millennia, producing not just man and our societies, but the vast and complex physical world that we inhabit, and a cosmos full of other scientific wonders. In this I see the hand of God. To paraphrase Einstein, I see the clock and wonder at the clockmaker.

Consider the laws of conservation of mass and energy in physics. How can anyone fail to marvel at the fact that matter cannot be created nor destroyed? Every atom in our universe that currently exists has existed from the very birth of the universe. Every particle on earth, the very atoms that form your body, and every bit of the world we see were formed at the start of the universe: each and every atom. Perhaps a few of the atoms that are now your body at some point in the future will be a cloud or a patch of grass; perhaps at some point in the distant past they were a drop of water in the vast, black seas, or the left toe of a brontosaur. Just as a note, I refer to "atoms" for the sake of simplicity, recognizing that the atom is no longer considered the smallest or only building block of matter, ala protons, neutrons, electrons, gluons, quarks, anti-matter, and perhaps dark matter, and so on.

Science cannot explain how matter came to be, but science confirms that matter *cannot* be created or destroyed by man or by the physics of the world we know. I recall a long-ago argument with a drug-addled guy. He groused that this law cannot be true because, "You know, like, if you cremate a body what is left is just ashes, man, nowhere near the same amount of matter. You know?" In my own drug-addled, though considerably better-educated, state, I explained that it was still an equal equation. "No dude, part of the body when it's burned hits the air and disperses, you know, as smoke and gas and as heat or energy." Once he stopped laughing about the "gas," he said he still felt it couldn't be true. But it is true. Atom for atom or particle for particle.

The remarkable fact of matter's indestructibility provides a powerful truth and further reason, for me, for faith. God, however you choose to define God, created matter and life. God made them, and they are everlasting. Whenever I doubt God's existence, I simply look around and wonder at the world and the extraordinary universe, and I know God

Cognitive Faith

must exist, because this all was created and has existed since the beginning.

Of course, this scientific fact also becomes a good news / bad news scenario when it comes to a hereafter. The good news is that the *atoms* that comprise your body, including those making up your brain and its miraculous electronic warehouse of memories and knowledge, will live on indefinitely. The bad news is that it is unlikely that your consciousness itself will. When people talk about being joyously reunited at death with loved ones or going to better place after death, they are hoping for some alternate reality or non-physical plane of existence that might capture or conserve consciousness. Of course, the possibility of an afterlife is a comforting thought. Sadly, such beliefs are based in non-scientific myths possibly springing from our animal instinct to covet survival, combined with the human intellectual ability to envision future states, real or imagined.

More interesting, and on some level more likely, might be a collective memory or consciousness. The simple fact of DNA and its again (helloooo?) miraculous and unerring coding for every plant and animal give some credence to the possibility of a similar and as-yet-undiscovered coding that has and continues to evolve within the atoms that we have, that life has, *that humans have*, utilized over the millennia. I find it intriguing to consider that the atoms we each borrow for our lifetimes might retain imprints or small bits of personal coding that over time have guided our evolution.

    Carl Jung proposed some interesting ideas on this topic when he wrote about inherited consciousness, which he referred to as the "collective unconscious." (*The Archetypes and the Collective Unconscious*, C.G. Jung, Princeton University Press, 1959) He compared collective consciousness to instincts, which are an accepted type of evolutionary coding we all seem to possess. But this other *consciousness*, according to Jung, exists beyond the conscious mind of individual awareness, beyond the personal unconscious or sub-conscious mind warehousing all individual memories and experiences, and beyond instinct. Instead "the contents of the collective unconscious have never been in consciousness, and therefore have never been individually acquired, but owe their existence exclusively to heredity." Jung spent considerable effort defining the content of the collective unconscious, proposing numerous "archetypes" at work influencing and creating some standardized human psychological schemes.

    The provocative part of Jung's theory is in the suggestion that we carry within us a unique ancestral identity or reincarnated coding, so that "the man of the past is alive in us today to a degree undreamt of before." Whether that coding can be confirmed or isolated by science, like DNA, is up for discussion, but, if isolated and deciphered, perhaps eventually we can unlock a key to capturing consciousness, maybe even eternal consciousness. This would be a great avenue of research for some progressive scientist to explore in the future.

Still, belief in an afterlife or eternal life, for me, remains in that realm of the mystical smoke-and-mirrors game that many religions play. They offer some later—after death or reincarnation—reward or punishment, as a carrot or stick to promote adherence to their faith. In the case of some religious sects, the afterlife rewards are quite impressive. Not just eternal life, but eternal life and a thousand virgins! Ultimately, I come back to evidence, and there is no credible scientific evidence of conscious life after death or of reincarnation, despite the great number of novels, movies, and television shows that tell stories to the contrary.

Newton's Laws

In the 1600s Isaac Newton, arguably the second most famous scientist in history, discovered, or perhaps better words would be tested and documented, a number of remarkable truths about our world. Loosely stated, Newton's First Law of physics says that force must be exerted to overcome inertia, and the Second Law says that a body in motion continues to move unless set upon by another force. Newton's Third Law states that force must be assessed in terms of action and reaction, or a magnitude of force being met with "equal and opposite" force, which represents another of science's conservation equations. I embrace the

Science

remarkable truth and simplicity of Newtonian physics. Of course, I also accept the paradoxical truths of chaos systems discussed in a later section.

In contemplating science and the relation of science to faith, I find Newtonian laws are foundational and deeply at work. Integrating these scientific concepts into faith takes some amount of explanation, so try to stay with me.

Thoughts and feelings occur as electro-chemical firings within our brains, which is to say that thoughts and feelings are forces. When thoughts or feeling occur, they utilize physical or chemical resources, and when the force of thought or feeling is exerted, it may result in action or in other thoughts or feelings. Because thoughts and feelings cannot be seen, per se, I think many people fail to recognize them as forces, as scientists failed for many years to see the invisible force of gravitation, until Newton tested and defined gravity as a force. On some level, however, we know that energy is expended when our thoughts and feelings occur. As a comparison, we easily understand that when we unplug our electronic devices, or the battery dies, our device can do no more computing until more energy is applied to make the computing possible. Our brains work like that. They consume energy to process thoughts and feelings.

Thoughts and feelings often translate into biological responses—sweaty palms, a smile, nervous movement—and sometimes into conscious or unconscious action. So, when we think or experience feelings about things, or when we take those conscious or unconscious actions, we *are* exerting or applying force or energy for movement in whatever direction the feeling, the thought, or the action is taking us. Once energy has been exerted mentally, or in moving in a given direction emotionally, or in movement physically, or even in movement spiritually, we create a momentum that is easier to continue than to change. Familiar thoughts easily move us in familiar directions. I will come back to this in a moment.

    Next, let's acknowledge that truly dire, inexplicable, or unlucky events happen to people every day. There are also happy, well-deserved, or lucky events happening as well. Natural catastrophes, miraculous near-misses, debilitating illness, career promotions, evil perpetrations, and lottery wins. Many, perhaps most, of these events are random and have no intrinsic intention. For example, all natural phenomena are neutral in intention. In general, we know not to consider a drought or a significant storm to be a personal message from the cosmos. Yet we sometimes exhibit the hubris of the unhumble when we shake our fist at the sky, blaming God for our personal misfortunes, our problems or our shortcomings. Or, for that matter, when we consider our good fortune to be a "blessing" from God. Even when evil or ill-willing people cross your path, following their own dark journey, there is no intention *from God* at work. God did not arrange to have these events harm you. Nor does God conspire to award you with good luck.

Likewise, much of the illness we encounter in life is not purposeful. Good or poor health is not intended as a gift nor as an affront. We do indeed have genetic differences that may predispose us to health or to illness. Over our lifetimes, we take actions or live in circumstances that may increase or decrease the likelihood of health, relationship, or career outcomes. The events of the world, the acts of others, and the action of biology on our life or the life of those close to us, these are simply the common occurrences of human life and should not be credited with divine meaning.

God did *not* imbue right or wrong into the events of the universe or our world, nor even into the events of your life or mine. Science tells us not to ascribe human attributes to that which is not human and has named such reasoning flaws anthropomorphism or personification. The tendency to see some events as good and some as bad, or "for us" or "against us," is to see them through a lens of human impact, or simply the impact to each of us personally. Theory of Mind, a psychological and philosophical proposition, states that humans naturally attribute human qualities to events, animals, and the world, because humans can only reflect on the outer world *through the filter of our human mind*. So, my interpretation of reality is based on what I see, what I think, and what I know—that is, what I have stored in my brain's memory banks—and how I feel. It is natural to judge events and our environment based on the filter of the human mind. It is nevertheless flawed reasoning.

Cognitive Faith

When we believe that God, luck, fortune, or any human construct is at work in the events of our lives, we run the risk of venturing into the realm of victims of circumstance, and this strips us of the true power we have been given. Rather, power, and indeed faith, enter this equation in our elevated and conscious "reaction" to events and circumstances. In another miraculous symmetry, Newton's very same laws defining the physical world also offer an individual path for tapping into those laws' power. When events in the world affect your life and seem to push you in a particular direction, there will be a reaction. There must be. You will naturally "move" based on the nature of the event: the angle of the hit, if you will. Newton's laws say you will be pushed and will then continue in that direction until a different force is exerted to move you in a different direction.

We have all known people who seem at the mercy of the events of their lives. Being in a 12-Step program, I have known many people with truly awful situations. I recall sitting with "Patti," a battered young woman wearing a patch over a damaged eye, the injury inflicted by her abusive boyfriend. She explained, "He was drinking, and he always gets so angry. And then he starts yelling. I try not to make him madder, but I can't leave. I know he is going to hit me, but I don't have any money, and my family hates him, and they won't help me. Then I drink or get high, too, because that's the only way I can cope." It is hard, when unjust events loom large in your life, to see that, even here, choice is at work. In fact, Patti had numerous choices available and the "reaction" she gave me was just one such choice. Patti did not stay sober, at least not at this juncture, and I do not know if she left the abusive boyfriend. I do not want to minimize her complex situation, but I can say, based on the fact that she was unable to pursue sobriety, that her stance, her reaction, her responding movement, did not provide sufficient force to move her in a different, healthier direction. To change direction from one path, especially an entrenched or powerfully pushed set of circumstances that is driving or impacting us, we are required to *exert or apply force*. If we do so, we can create new momentum going a different direction.

This is known in psychology as exercising free will. We can do something new. We can continue to follow our previous path. Or we can do nothing. There are many possible actions that might be taken. But choice is indeed at work here.

The Take Control Model and Free Will

In the many years since securing firm footing in recovery, I have spent most of my career either in corporate training roles or as an independent training consultant, developing and delivering course material on a wide variety of business topics. One course I designed and deliver is called Emotional Intelligence at Work. I mention the course because it includes a section on a helpful model called the "Take Control Model." The model is a simple methodology for improving behavior related to emotions.

Cognitive Faith

We all know that at work, or in our personal lives for that matter, negative emotional displays or emotional responses can strain productivity and relationships. The goal of the Take Control Model is to improve or minimize these undesirable emotional displays or responses. However, the goal cannot be to eliminate emotions. Emotions don't work that way. In fact, emotions cannot be commanded by any human being. We cannot tell ourselves to feel a given emotion. For example, if I look at you and say, "Feel joy now!" can you will it to be so? No. Nor can you command anger, fear, frustration, or any emotion. Emotions come upon us. Some emotions can be "triggered" by particular events or circumstances. While both positive and negative emotions can be triggered, generally we refer to triggering in reference to the more unpleasant or unproductive emotions. Sometimes triggers are predictable, and people with better emotional intelligence know their personal triggers. These people, whether from innate emotional intelligence or through learned self-management, cope with unwanted emotional responses by making behavioral adjustments or, in some cases, by prudently avoiding triggering situations.

However, many common triggers simply cannot be avoided. For example, traffic is a common trigger situation for many people, and, in the extreme, results in road rage. In parenting, overly loud or hyperactive child play is a common trigger. You simply cannot choose not to drive in traffic or stay entirely away from your children. In business, you might be triggered by the way a co-worker talks in meetings, or by

Science

the time and paperwork required for a needed order. Again, you cannot simply refuse to attend business meetings or do without the supplies you are ordering. You have to face these situations, even knowing you may end up experiencing a negative emotional response. Unchecked, the negative emotional response may lead to negative thoughts, for example, of how much you hate listening to that person, or how frustrated you are having to wait for approval for your workplace needs. The negative thoughts reinforce the negative feeling. The negative feeling combined with the reinforcing negative thoughts can lead to displays of your negative emotional state, for example: rolling your eyes, making audible sighs, or, worse, saying negative words or exhibiting other unseemly behavior. As you might imagine, for people with actual anger-management issues, triggered negativity can result in some very bad behavior. (See Fig. 2)

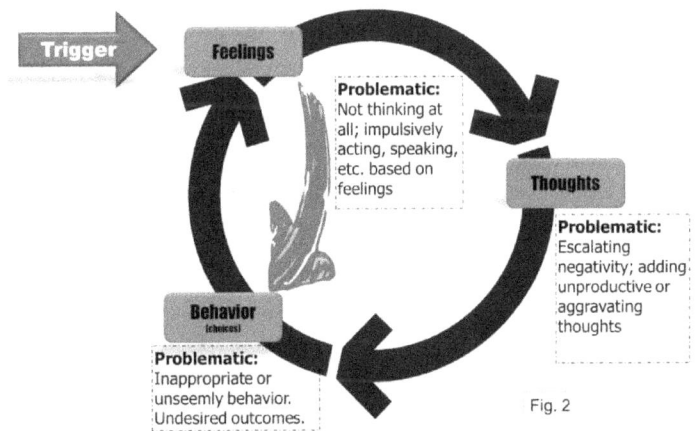

Fig. 2

Cognitive Faith

In trainings, at this point, many people acknowledge how commonly they experience such situations. They admit to regularly feeling negative emotions and entertaining negative thoughts, and accept that their behavior may indeed reflect that inner negativity. In fact, because situations that trigger negative emotions are so prevalent, many people spend countless minutes or even hours daily in the vicious cycle of being triggered into loops of negative emotional responses, thoughts, and behaviors. When unchecked, these negative emotional responses can have an intensifying or escalating effect.

While emotions cannot be commanded, by contrast, we can all summon a thought. So, when a wave of negative feeling comes upon a person, a person can *at any point choose to interject a thought that will not escalate or feed the negative feeling*. This consciously chosen thought is called a *neutralizing thought*. That neutral thought can actually *de-escalate* the feeling at the base of the negativity. The thought need not be Pollyannaish, it need not even be positive, but anyone can select a thought that is neutral. In traffic, if someone cuts you off, instead of "that IDIOT!" and punching your gas pedal to ride up on the person's bumper, you can, at any point, chose to think instead, "Well, that wasn't very smart." Or, if you get really good at it: "I hope she doesn't hurt someone driving like that." In behavioral treatment of anger issues, the person might write down some sample neutralizing thoughts on a card and keep that card at the ready for anger-triggering situations. When the rage comes upon them, all they have to do is choose to read the neutralizing-thought statement. (See Fig. 3)

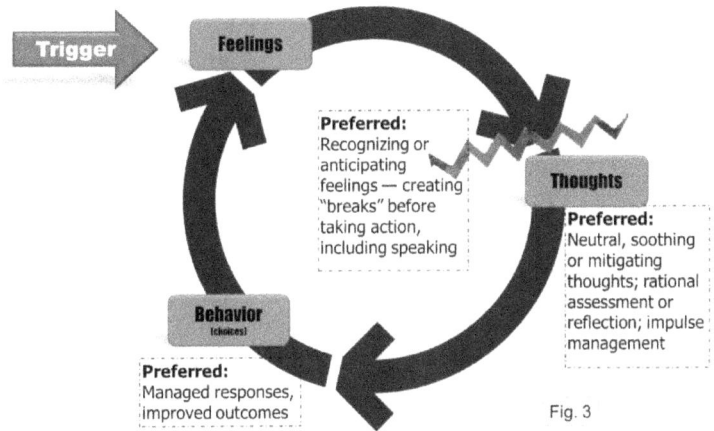

Fig. 3

The amazing part is that the brain accepts the unemotional thought and adjusts the person's emotions to align with this indifferent view of the situation. Obviously, the subsequent behavior will also then be improved. The key is to take control of the thoughts, and then the thoughts will take control of the emotional responses. For people with anger issues, this can be like a miracle. For the rest of us, it is still a powerful tool for managing unproductive or negative emotions. It is no longer acceptable to say "I can't help how I feel."

This is very good news. Our thoughts, reactions, and actions can provide the force to alter the direction of our lives. Or, sadly, we can also reinforce or carry on under the momentum of negative triggers from the external world. But we have been given the power to choose, to think, to manage our emotional reactions, and to take different or new action. When we do so purposefully, we can then change the trajectory of our lives.

So where does faith come into this equation? When conducting training in a corporate setting, I cannot mention that adding the power of faith to the process enhances the results, but I can here. I am not a rageaholic, but I have definitely had, and still have, deeply rooted triggers. Most of my triggers relate to feelings of inadequacy or insecurity but manifest in defiance, defensiveness, and arrogance, with a little dash of flight syndrome. Being from a lower-income, unsophisticated family, I found corporate-world interactions very stressful, especially as I advanced through the ranks and interacted with more senior corporate leadership. I knew that I was smart, that I had a good education, and that I was technically capable, but those underlying feelings kept resulting in displays of unseemly workplace behavior. For example, in the early years of my career, I was sent home from a job for inappropriate workplace dress. In a later role, I was written up for excessive use of profanity. I was fired from *two different jobs* for challenging leaders. I quit jobs because I felt slighted. Intellectually, I understood, usually after the fact, that I had behaved improperly. But my emotions and underlying insecurities were driving my behavior, reinforced by thoughts of defiance or defensiveness.

Over the years, I explored various strategies to improve my performance, both in my career and my dysfunctional relationships. In therapy, I identified some of the underlying issues, as mentioned earlier, particularly feelings of inadequacy. I also attended some self-help seminars. Of course, I worked my 12-Step program and spent time with an insightful "sponsor." Even so, I struggled and made only slow progress. Verbally and in my heart, I wanted to improve and navigate toward more significant business and financial success and happier relationships. *I needed to take control but, to be honest, taking control was not easy for me.* I, like a rageaholic, was trying to overcome some deep-rooted, self-sabotaging patterns.

As a therapist recommended, for years I did daily written affirmations. Slowly, I developed the ability to insert more positive thoughts into my self-defeating mind. But the real key was found and real change started for me when I reinforced my affirmations with faith, and, as we will discuss later, the action of faith, which is prayer. (See Fig. 4)

So, to re-cap, through free will we can take control of unhealthy thoughts and feelings, and have better outcomes. And, if we repeat or habitualize making those better choices, we create momentum that will make better choices still easier.

Cognitive Faith

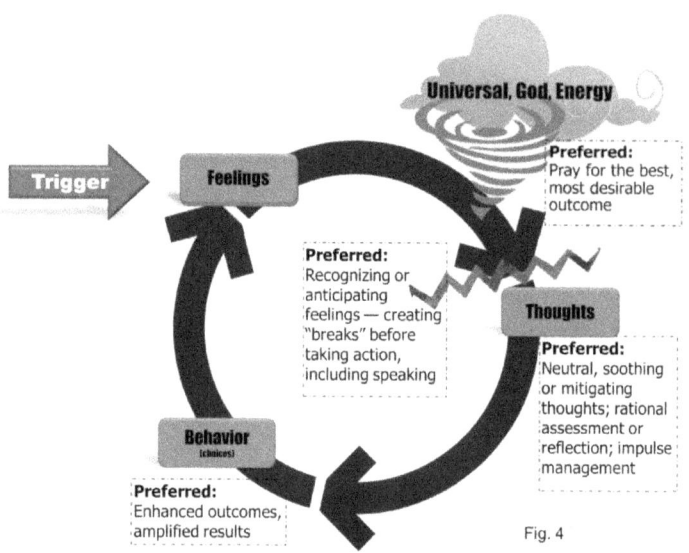

Fig. 4

    This is an extremely important concept. I now see how this concept was at work when I walked away, with great difficulty and uncertainty, from drug and alcohol abuse all those years ago. This concept helps me, even today, stay sober and on a path of positive forward momentum. As I mentioned above, once the initial force has been applied to change, it is easier to continue and maintain momentum than it is to push in a new direction at the outset.

    God is not, however, orchestrating the good or the bad circumstances of your life. Humans have the ability to choose how to respond, to exert force, and to reap the rewards of a new direction, or not. This is not only true for people with drug or alcohol problems. This concept provides instruction to any person who would like to feel empowered or wants to make a change or an improvement in any area of their life: relationships, health, career, or emotional stability. Any area. I will also say as a spoiler that the action-reaction equation when dealing with human choice and circumstances is not a simple zero-sum situation.

Does God Love Man and Plan Our Lives?

You might be asking yourself right now: Does God care at all about us then? Did God simply create the world and the laws of physics, and abandon us to our own devices and fates? This is a troubling question indeed, especially for those steeped in a religious upbringing or spiritual rhetoric about God loving you and all people. The answer I have to this question may be hard to hear. Even so, I feel that answer is immeasurably better than the answers I got from Christianity along the way.

In church, I was told that God watches over, cares about, and has a plan for each and every one of us. While God's reasons are unknowable, according to the church *everything* that occurs is indeed part of God's divine plan. So, *every* event in my life, and the life of *every* other person, is part of God's plan. Bummer. The implication of this reasoning is God actually intends for some people to die in horrible ways. That God intends to have evil-doers perpetrate atrocities against innocent people. That God intended for the vast majority of our human population to be unsaved.

God's personal interest in and individual plans for each of us are simply another of the unlikely stories religious pundits tell us. Early on I recognized this as a paradox. God was said to be all-powerful. Check. God was said to deeply love every person and is watching over our lives. Check. However, very bad things happen to people all the time. Even to very good people. Humm. Why didn't God just keep the bad stuff from happening? I recall a well-intentioned pastor trying to give me an explanation of why evil exists and bad things happen. He stated that it all started with the Garden of Eden and Eve succumbing to temptation. So, God removed humans from the perfect place, the place with no evil and no illness, and now here we are! But even at a young age, I recall asking, "If Eden was perfect and safe and all good, why was the Devil there?"

Einstein said, "I believe in Spinoza's God, who reveals himself in the orderly harmony of what exists, not in a God that concerns himself with the fates and actions of human beings." And, "the idea of a personal God is an anthropological concept which I am unable to take seriously." (*The Cosmic View of Albert Einstein*, edited by Walt Martin and Magda Ott, 2013)

For me, too, the humanistic God of the church was logically flawed. I found myself struggling with belief in God, because the religious definition of God and all the trappings of religion did not make sense. In this struggle, of wanting spiritual faith but finding religion wanting, I was not alone.

Part Two
Religion

Religion, Historically

When I was completing my undergraduate degree in anthropology, one course I took explored the topic of culture and religion. Religion, my professor asserted, or some version of it, has been part of every human culture. From rudimentary forms of religion among the earliest hunters and gatherers living in caves, cliff-sides, or huts, to complex institutional religions catering to modern-day humans living in apartments, homes or mansions. The cultural function of religion in any case is threefold. First, religion provides an explanation of the world, including its origins and physical workings. Second, religion defines morality and behavioral prescriptions for the culture. Finally, religion gives comfort, quelling fear, easing the hearts and minds of its adherents, and giving assurance of the meaningfulness of our lives.

Explaining the World's Workings

Early man had no explanations for the physical workings of nature. Surely they wondered at everyday events. That the sun brings light every day. That the seasons unerringly progress over a year. That the stars bedazzle the nighttime skies. Surely, they were heartsick over tragedies and hardships universally part of the human experience. The painful death of a child. The destruction of food sources by a freak act of nature, an earthquake, a flood, a terrifying hurricane. Since the earliest communication took place between humans, human beings have shared their own unique explanations of the world and life's events through their cultural lore and religion. Their stories explained why it was so and what it all means. It is not surprising, it is even reasonable, that for the first few eons of human existence, religion generally answered the question of the workings of the world with the knowable or unknowable will of personified or naturalistic "gods."

Evolutionarily, some scholars attribute the emergence of naturalistic gods and stories about those gods' influence on human life to the development of higher human mental capacities. Empathy, the ability to mentally put oneself into a consideration of how another person might think or feel, has been cited in particular. Theory of Mind psychology, the human tendency to view the world through the filter of a human understanding or viewpoint, also supports the empathy explanation of how our Gods have been defined. While we could not know with certainty what another person, or animal, thinks, feels, or knows, early man could and did project assumptions about their possible thoughts and feelings onto them.

      Early on, the human species developed this unique mental capacity to reflect on, consider, or care about what other humans might be experiencing or thinking, and this capacity is known as empathy. With this capability, early humans are thought to have naively extended empathetic readings into all their surroundings, attributing human feelings and intentions to animals, inanimate objects, and even environmental events. Hence, a mountain watches over us, a hurricane was due to an angry sea, or the jealous she-wolf took a child because she wanted to be a mother, etc. Eventually, the stories and characteristics attributed to the entities expanded and evolved, with humans adding backstories and personalities that became for the various early human tribes their cultures' unique polytheistic entities and lore. Thus, the wolf represented one spirit god, the sun another, the wind, the sea, and the mountain others, and so on.

      In relatively recent human history, that is, in the past few thousand years, particularly with the evolution of writing, anthropologists and historians have collected quite clear documentation of numerous cultures practicing such naturalistic and polytheistic brands of theology. We have clear descriptions of their detailed mythologies and quite complex religious rituals, practiced to appease or influence the entities or curry favor in one or another entity's purview. Familiar examples include the ancient Greek, Roman, and Asian mythologies, and the many and varied religious creeds of the North, Central, and South American Indian tribes.

      While naturalistic, polytheistic religion is thought to have existed in the earliest human cultures, monotheist theology and modern religions—Judaism, Christianity, and Islam most notably—are more recent human creeds. Still, the explanations for the workings of the world, and the intricacies of these religions' rituals, in a very elementary respect offer little difference from those of the naturalistic, or polytheistic faiths. In the final analysis, they still present a credo that rolls up the hows and whys of the world to the doings of a humanistic entity, now simply their "One God." Like the primitive archetypes, each modern religion includes its own careful version or story of creation. Each provides an explanation of the natural world and its history, most supplying some imaginative and miraculous flourishes. Each religion involves complex rituals, and the human congregants, through performance of those rituals, aspire to appease and win favor with their God.

Religion

Of Two Minds – Conflicting Beliefs

As the Ages of Reason and Enlightenment dawned, in the 1500s to 1700s, scientific discoveries emerged and progressed over time to our current level of scientific understanding. However, most of the increasingly dominant western religions, over the same few hundred years, did not adjust their stories to allow for scientific discoveries. Most remained dogmatic and substantially stood by their texts and mystical components, even those that defied increasingly accepted contrary knowledge. Religious belief and scientific belief began to stand apart. In some cases, scientific explanations or revelations that conflicted with religious beliefs were suppressed or denied by the religiously minded power bases. Galileo was placed under arrest by the Inquisition for the suggestion that the world was not the center of the universe. Darwin's evolutionary theories were refuted and disdained by Christianity and still are in some religious circles. The entire fields of paleontology and archeology have been denied or questioned. As the chasm between religious beliefs and scientific knowledge has grown, followers of religious doctrine have been forced either to deny scientific truths or to be "of two minds."

"Kathy," a woman I have chatted with, a devout Catholic, simply says she does not even try to reconcile the teachings of her church with the scientific realities she also generally accepts. "It is not something I think much about," she said. She simply refused to open any discussion about possible conflicts between her religious beliefs and science

Cognitive Faith

facts. "But I will say this," she finally said. "I go to church every week and I rarely have a thought about science."

Another man I questioned, Dr. J., a Protestant physician, said quite reasonably that he takes what he can use from the church and the Bible and disregards the rest. When I asked him about creation of the world in six days, he said with a self-satisfied smile, "Well, I just look at it as God days. God days might very well be a billion years, who knows?" He obviously had used that response before. To see how far his personal amendments to scripture might go, I asked Dr. J. about Jesus being the literal son of God and only path to everlasting life, Immaculate Conception, and the resurrection. Now the smile faded. I was clearly making him uncomfortable. "Look," he replied, somewhat exasperated, "if you are going to push me about whether I believe all of the New Testament is literally true, I guess I will just say yes. It is my religion. I do believe." I wanted to then ask about how his beliefs jibe with the biological and medical sciences, but I knew asking would have been argumentative.

I think it is safe to say that many people may feel the discomfort of belonging to a religion that presents a text and world view that conflict with scientific knowledge. In psychology, this schism between beliefs which conflict with each other is referred to as cognitive dissonance. Now, I am not suggesting that all people who subscribe to a religion blindly accept as literal truth every fantastical story and unwaveringly agree with every tenet presented within their religion. Far from it. I believe it is *more common*, as in the two examples above, to live with the ambiguity inherent in acceptance of and observance of religion, and rational acceptance of scientific fact and common-sense reality. People are simply rarely pushed, as I began pushing the doctor above, to try to reconcile the conflicts between the two systems of beliefs. Most can and do rather neatly compartmentalize the two, taking comfort and joy from their religious beliefs without wanting or needing to disbelieve the scientific facts or everyday reality they live with day to day. As I shared earlier, for me, the disparity between religious beliefs and tenets and real-world reality was simply irreconcilable, but clearly many people quite capably manage the incongruity.

So, is there a problem with having conflicting beliefs? In reality, people *commonly* hold assorted beliefs that if compared or closely examined might produce uncomfortable cognitive dissonance. Virtually every person has such conflicting beliefs, and religion or faith-based issues are only one possibility. For example, it is not uncommon for a person to believe our government is entirely too involved and restrictive in our lives, and that we pay too much in taxes. At the same time, that same person may look at the social issues of homelessness, crime, traffic, pollution, healthcare, or whatever, and lament that the government needs to "do something." We might enjoy actively using the Internet to engage with family and friends on social media, correspond over email, manage personal finances, and shop online, and at the same time lament the social isolation that electronic devices have brought about. Or a person can believe in the importance of saving or making investments for a secure future, and also believe in pampering themselves and their family today, because life is short, and you have to live life fully in the moment, as you could die tomorrow.

While common, a few important points can be made about conflicting beliefs. One, not every person is willing to recognize or acknowledge that they have conflicting beliefs. Some people prefer to insist all their beliefs are certain, logical, and, of course, correct. I like that in school debate courses or competitions the participants may have to argue either side of the issue. Debate rules force the students to understand both sides of a given argument and to engage their analytical thinking, recognizing flaws or conflicts on either side of a subject. For myself, I recognize how I at turns argue as a reasonable, if restrained, conservative with some of my extremely liberal friends, then at other times argue vehemently for social systems and reforms with acquaintances who are conservatives. I realize I may appear or actually be speaking at odds with myself. But, importantly, I try to *reflect on* my political beliefs and acknowledge that some of my beliefs or positions may seem to or actually conflict—or need to evolve. My beliefs are multifaceted, dynamic, and always subject to revision based on new information.

Two, even if you rationally accept your conflicting beliefs, you may be confronted with choices or decisions at points where you will *be required* to take a stand, so to speak, on one side or the other, based on your beliefs. For example, if you believe, on one hand, that cities should be able to maintain housing-density restrictions in residential neighborhoods to preserve quality-of-life standards, but also recognize that, as a social issue, some areas desperately need additional housing, you may be confronted with a ballot measure that proposes adjustments to city-density restrictions. How you vote, of course, will be left to your overriding value. But, at that point, your two conflicting ideas have been presented to you in a form where you will have to decide which belief is more important for you to abide by.

This is true, perhaps more dramatically, with conflicts in religious beliefs. Many people earnestly engage with a specific religion and also may hold values or ideas that may conflict with some of its tenets. Like Dr. J. above, a believer can theoretically accept or hold both beliefs indefinitely without a forced belief face-off. Still, over time, life events may, and often do, present situations that will test adherent's support of one or the other side of these beliefs.

Challenges that force belief showdowns may be presented in a variety of circumstances. Do you sign that petition supporting a position for or against one of the conflicting beliefs? Do you agree to picket or protest a place or a group with your co-parishioners? Do you vote for or against that legislation? Do you donate to a cause that is pro or against one side or the other of the conflicting belief set? Do you support that candidate that has clearly espoused beliefs, again, for or against your religion's tenets, knowing that they will indeed be actively advocating for their espoused position and thereby supporting or obstructing one side of your beliefs?

      These choices actionably challenge your willingness to take a stand, nominally or otherwise, on one side or the other of your conflicted beliefs. More personally and stealthily, you may be faced with deciding to hire or promote a person who is overtly aligned with or opposed to a given belief at work, or, still more personally, make decisions when a family member or close friend puts you into an actionable situation. Do you attend that friend's gay marriage ceremony? Do you accept that out-of-wedlock child into your family? Do you support turning off that life-support machine as requested by your favorite aunt? Still, in these cases, the individual will make their choices as private, personal matters.

      The dissonance periodically becomes a public matter, however, when specific groups attempt to advance or impose their beliefs through social or political forums, advocating for their beliefs with behavioral or social prescriptions for the general population: for example, when literalists campaign to have creationism taught at schools on an equal footing with evolution, when a particular sect mounts opposition to legal marriage for gays, or in any case where a religious majority or powerful faction attempts to impose its "moral" restrictions onto an entire population.

While I suspect that many members even within those religious advocacy groups might quietly hold more moderate positions on the topics, it is nevertheless disturbing to see and hear proponents unyieldingly asserting their belief as unequivocally right and true. When matters come to such a point on the political or social-action front, moderate believers may be trapped, like my physician friend, into taking what can only be seen as an uncomfortable and, to rational thinkers untenable, stand.

Still, it is safe to say, in today's modern world, in most cases, even among followers, religion is no longer turned to as the source of truth in the physical workings of the world or for explanations of how the world came to be.

Prescribing Morality and Behavior

Over the millennia of human existence, behavior prescriptions have also been defined within religion. What behavior is right and what behavior is wrong, how marriage and lineage are managed, and the consequences of wrong-doing. Whether dictated by an early shaman and or a medieval church cleric, in human society religious doctrine has traditionally defined the codes of conduct for the flock. Governance, another topic of anthropology, is largely inseparable from religion over the greatest portion of human existence. From earliest times, definitions of right and wrong behavior and the consequences for wrong-doing were adjudicated by the culture's clergy in concert with the societal leadership, at least until very recent history, as discussed below. The prescription of behavior by religious canons undoubtedly provided, and may still be argued to provide, an important moral compass and guide for social decorum. I would venture to say that a significant percentage of most religious prescriptions for behavior are indeed reasonable and good.

On the other hand, if much is reasonable and good, then naturally one must say that at least some of the tenets or prescriptions for behavior based in religion are not so reasonable and good. Among the most problematic and widespread of tenets is religious supremacy, that is, the concept that my religion is the best religion, the one true religion, or the only true path to God and salvation. Some religions take it further, actually condemning other belief systems and their adherents. Often, the condemnation includes a penalty. Those people practicing "the wrong" religion may be damned to eternal hellfire. While postmortem damnation is an awful curse, more immediate and infinitely more common is the treatment of non-subscribers as *less than* or inferior to the favored religion's followers.

I am not meaning to imply a conscious conspiracy to divide people and devalue some, but typically the largest western religions do just that, sometimes even within sub-sets of their own denominations. This us versus them or better than or inferior religious dichotomy has spawned some ugly divisiveness and unseemly attitudes of superiority, and has even become the basis of human wars, all in the strangely ironic guise of moral rightness. We have seen this evil in one tribe conducting murderous raids on neighbors who worshipped the sun god instead of the wind, in early Christians persecuted for failure to recognize the Roman gods, in Christians slaughtering the godless savages in the New World, in Catholics fighting the Protestants or the opposite, and in radical Muslims bombing Jewish synagogues or vice versa. To be clear, the rationale of religious rightness need not involve killing to be unkind, harmful, and even dangerous, and indeed the subtler varieties of condemnation or marginalization are much more prevalent.

    I do not wish to discount the numerous good services that many religious groups strive to provide. Doing charitable work, feeding or housing the poor, bringing aid to underprivileged or devastated countries, and so forth, are good and worthy activities often undertaken by religious sects. Where the religious charity-workers or missionaries sometimes go astray, I think, is in the underlying mission of conversion. The recipients of the charitable services are encouraged to believe, or come to believe, as the church helping them believes. The people being helped, it is thought, are most helped when they are saved by the beliefs of the charitable religious group. Where conversion and recruitment underlie good works, the selflessness of the charity is somewhat undermined.

    Judgments within religion go beyond simple attitudes of religious superiority, however. Many religions also condemn common behaviors. Among some commonly judged: divorce, birth control, homosexuality, drinking alcohol, meat-eating, sex or co-habitation outside of marriage, and polygamy. The list, of course, is unique for each religion, with some religions providing long and particular lists. No zippers for the Amish. No haircuts for the Hasidic Jews. No visible skin other than eyes for a woman in strict Muslim communities. Some of the prescriptive beliefs are quant or harmless to outsiders. But others are hot-beds for governmental or societal debates, including marriage rights, right-to-die issues, pacifism, and abortion, to name just a few.

Indeed, adhering to religious dictates may be challenging even to the members of the religion, and this in some cases becomes the basis of non-conformity or attrition. Still, the traditions, restrictions, or even judgment and consequences for behavioral prescriptions administered among the adherents of a religion, that is, for those *who choose* to engage in the religion, is their own business. The problems arise when adherents judge or seek to punish those who breach their doctrines *outside their religion*. Or when religious believers actively attempt to force others to believe as they do through political or coercive activities.

Behavioral dictates in the last century or two in many modern cultures have, however, become less and less associated with religion. Governance, laws, and social mores are thought, at least theoretically, to better provide uniform prescriptions for acceptable behavior to large groups, especially those societies with significant diversity in religion and culture. The doctrines of a dominant religion may underpin legal and social norms, as Christianity does in the United States, but in most modern nations today, the church is not invited to the political table, at least not overtly. The philosophy of separation of church and state has been adopted explicitly or implicitly in many counties in the hope of promoting improved tolerance and fairness, and to protect of the rights of both large and small factions. In those places where strict religious doctrines continue to serve as social, political, and even in some places legal prescriptions, the problems of marginalization, condemnation, and subjugation of outliers is inevitably heightened.

Another early reader of this manuscript argued with me about whether political separation actually exists, even in nations that espouse it. He insisted that most countries are still troublingly influenced by religious-belief systems and continue to produce religiously constrained and sometimes prejudiced legislation. He cited stem-cell research, GMO crop and stock research and even Artificial Intelligence research opposition here in the United States due to specific religious ideologies that have successfully hobbled progress in these fields. I agree with the concern and think his argument further supports my comments rather than refutes them. Just to qualify: religious ideologies and agendas do continue to wield influence in the United States and other modern countries, even those that espouse separation of church and state. My point is more that we need to support and embody this separation of interests if we are to coexist, and that the concept, as recognized by many contemporary cultures, is critical. Believe what you believe, and abide by your beliefs, but society at large must be governed with tolerance and a broader view.

    We now live in a world of mass communication, where cultural behaviors around the globe are readily visible. The dichotomy between peaceful co-existence in some areas where people have different religious beliefs or faiths, versus the observable unpleasantness seen in areas dominated by religious zealotry or disputatious religious dogma, again becomes anathema to moderate sensibilities.

    We see both versions of culture right here in the United States. On social media I saw a video clip not long ago of a white American driver yelling vile and inaccurate racial and religious epithets at an Asian driver. The Asian driver was, incidentally, a US veteran and Christian. Shocking, but unfortunately not an isolated case. More recently I attended an out of state wedding, and at the hotel where we stayed another wedding was taking place, a lovely, joyful Pakistan wedding. I was horrified to hear someone muttering in the lobby about the "dot heads" taking over the hotel (and yes, that was another error; the festivities were Muslim, not Hindi – so, no dots). This is not to imply that religiosity is the only source of societal narrow-mindedness. Many secular groups, or even entire governments, have advocated for divisive principles or doctrines to justify unsavory behavior, including genetic superiority, economic entitlement, and nationalistic supremacy. That religious zealotry and religious intolerance continue to be a present, visible and disruptive force, simply reflects one more reason for many to turn away from formal religion.

Giving Comfort and Peace

What then of comfort? What then of the balm to the soul? If science explains the workings of the world better than religion, if secular governance and cultural mores more fairly address the prescriptions for acceptable and lawful behavior, does religion have a meaningful role in modern society? Does faith? Comfort may well be the last bastion of religion.

Currently, over 23% of the US population identifies as agnostic, atheist or "nothing" for religious affiliation. And that number is growing. Approximately 26% of the population never attends religious services, and another 20% attend services either less than twice a year or less than once a year (*The Association of Religious Data Archives*, theARDA.com, 2017). The trend is clearly away from religious associations and particularly away from the formal practice of religion through church attendance. The question is: do humans, having had some form of religion as an elemental component of culture from the earliest days, need anything that religion offers in today's world? Are we humans, in backing away from religion, losing something?

Cognitive Faith

One of my in-laws, whom I will call "Fred," is a Catholic and regular church-goer. In his sixties, Fred confides that he liked church better when the sermon was in Latin. "I used to sit in the pew and listen to the sermon without having to think too deeply about what it was about. There was incense, chanting the responses, the singing, and, well, not a lot of thinking. It was calming." Many church-goers I have spoken with share their enjoyment of the rituals of their religion. Well-known words, bowing heads, songs. More than a few have stated that the best parts of their religious attendance are not the edicts, strict lessons, and judgments, but rather the joyful times, the celebrations, weddings, christenings, holiday services. Or they simply enjoy revisiting favorite stories or passages from their scriptures. I think again of Dr. J., who could take what he could use and leave the rest.

Still, as discussed, there is a significant migration away from church-going. Other soul-soothing activities are, however, gaining in popularity. According to a 2013 article in the *Huffington Post*, yoga has become a 27-billion-dollar industry in the US, "a panacea for the ailments of modern society — tech overload, disconnection and alienation, insomnia, stress and anxiety." ("How Yoga Became a 27 Billion Dollar Industry," Carolyn Gregoire, Huffington Post, December 2013) Still, most US yoga focuses on the physical exercises, whereas the full practice of yoga involves more spiritual elements. The five-thousand-year-old practice involves "stilling the thoughts of the mind in order to experience one's true self, and ultimately, to achieve liberation (*moksha*) from the cycle of birth and death (*samsara*), or enlightenment."

Similarly, mindfulness is derived from a deep and robust Buddhist practice but reduced in contemporary western circles to an almost religionless spiritual practice. No need for exercise: one simply seeks attentiveness to one's inner world and purposeful attentiveness to one's outer world. The practice of mindfulness is rapidly growing in popularity, and trendy institutions that guide members to embrace mindfulness are currently capitalizing on its popularity.

So, it does seem that the need for a balm of comfort and peace, that my in-law eloquently described, is on some level with us still. The question becomes, can just anything do the trick? Chanting, meditation, deep breathing, communing with nature, extreme sports, video games, watching TV, playing with electronic devices, even working? If traditional religion is failing for so many of us, can humankind simply forfeit the need for the comforts of faith? Is modern human life truly an existential journey that gets only the random momentary reprieve of a "downward dog" to quell the disquiet we might feel? If faith has a place, I think it must offer more. More than passing moments of peace of mind. More than fantastical beliefs. More than a set of rules with dire consequences.

Cognitive Faith

I certainly found that I needed more from faith. And, I had a lot on the line with this faith question. As a recovering addict and alcoholic, I had no desire to allow drugs or alcohol to retake my life. I had *years* of vivid experience living a shabby life staunchly disavowing faith and God. And I also had *years* of trying *and failing* to stay away from or manage my drug and alcohol use. Recovery, for me, is serious business, perhaps life and death. And recovery requires that I enlist or tap into power beyond my own.

While I managed to hobble together a few years of precarious sobriety based on stroppy faith, I knew that, without a comfortable faith, I was putting my sobriety and my hope for a healthy, productive life at risk. The 12-Step recovery program offers a simple, even elegant, definition of their requisite spiritual belief with the phrasing "God as you understand God." While the phrasing was designed to offer inclusiveness for all brands of religion and faith, it became for me much more. It was an open door for me to craft my own unique idea of faith, that is, Cognitive Faith.

The Real Value of Faith

If, over the eons, the purpose of religious faith has been to explain the world, to dictate behavior, and to offer comfort, and if each of these functions might as well be served through science, government, and individual leisure activities respectively, is there a reason to pursue faith at all? This question is valid, and many in today's world are indeed embracing a world without faith, God, or spirituality. I believe, as discussed, this rejection of faith is largely based on the failure of *religion* to remain relevant in today's world as the vehicle for the delivery of faith and understanding of God.

But the relevance or irrelevance of religion should not be the basis for a decision to have or not have faith in or a relationship with God. Therefore, I propose three good reasons for embracing faith. First, the exercise of reaching out to God and tapping into spirituality fills your heart and soul. Admittedly, this is the weakest of reasons, because, as already discussed, people today have many options for soul-soothing activities, including yoga, communing with nature, mindfulness, etc. But I would argue that there is a *significant* difference, a *substantial* elevation of the comfort and peace received, when one is directing the activity toward God consciousness, rather than simply doing the activity for relaxation or stress relief.

The second and infinitely more compelling reason for faith is that seeking and engaging with God can empower you. That is to say, God's power is accessible. It is accessed through faith and purposeful engagement with God. In the coming section, we cover "how to" access and engage God's power, but here let me assert that doing so can strengthen you, improve your abilities in selected areas, and produce desired changes. Now, to be clear, I make no promises here for miracles. No stories of lotteries won or spontaneous healing. Nor will I say unequivocally that a miraculous change cannot happen. But more often, and more likely, are changes or improvement of the incremental variety. God's power can simply strengthen you, making you more capable.

Upon reflection, I believe it is this second benefit of faith and belief in God that makes recovery from addiction issues possible. People who do not have substance-abuse problem or are otherwise endowed with a natural and unerring sense of right direction, may not understand this benefit. But not all of us innately possess this capability. In fact, I would estimate that a substantial percentage of humans *do not* possess an infallible internal compass that always moves them away from unhealthy or counterproductive behavior and toward the better path or the path leading toward their innermost desired futures.

Not a Level Playing Field

In the book *Hillbilly Elegy: A Memoir of a Family and Culture in Crisis* by J.D. Vance, (Harper, 2016), the author shares insight into the history of his family and their saga. His family was from a rural area in the Kentucky Appalachians and later immigrated to blue-collar Ohio. Vance describes the engrained lifestyle patterns he saw within his family and among his people, the hillbillies: patterns that have led to persistent cycles of poverty, abuse, and alcoholism.

The themes in *Hillbilly Elegy* resonated with me. Our family was significantly poorer than most other families in our middle-class, Los Angeles-area home town. Growing up, my clothes came from secondhand stores. We lived in a rented house, where the roof leaked in the rain, and where having the gas, electricity, or telephone temporarily turned off was not uncommon. My mother worked as a secretary and left the house early to catch a bus to work and did not return until evening. Her meager salary had to provide for four kids, my father having disappeared from our lives. As a consequence, we were all a bit unkempt, often unsupervised, and were somewhat lacking in social refinements. I had never been inside a nice department store, on an airplane, or to a restaurant with cloth napkins, until I was an adult. I never joined a club in school, never attended a football game, and never went to a high school dance, let alone a prom. No one at home discussed the value of extracurricular activities, college choices or careers with me, ever. I compare this to a conversation I recently overheard in a conference room involving a leader in my company I will call "Frank."

"My son, Mason, is doing a project on investing in the stock market." Frank shared. "He told me his portfolio was doing pretty well, so I asked him if he had invested in our company's stock." Knowing our company stock was a bit down in recent weeks, Frank smiled as he shared the punch line: "The kid tells me yeah, he did invest in our company, but he was still doing great, because he shorted our stock!" His son, Mason, was thirteen at that point.

In some ways, the game *is* fixed. When you come from the sticks of Kentucky, or the inner city, or even, like me, as one of the kids from a poor family in a middle-class neighborhood, it can be harder to exercise thoughtful,

Cognitive Faith

reasonable thinking and find a path toward success and happiness. Some people have the edge, from an early age, of being exposed to prestigious schools, successful parents, and thoughtful discourse representing elevated mental functioning and, apparently, a well-balanced stock portfolio. Others of us struggle, having been raised in insecure, unsophisticated, or unhealthy environments. While people can and do rise above such challenges, it *is* something to be overcome. It is also a challenge that people raised without such shackles may not understand.

    I listened to a speaker at an AA meeting I will call "Barry" not long ago. Barry was raised in South Central Los Angeles. He said, "Everyone I knew growing up drank excessively, used drugs, and was involved in gangs or crime." Barry won a baseball scholarship to college, but despite the opportunity and an eventual short-lived professional baseball career, struggled with aligning his admittedly uncivilized social behavior with the auspicious prospects of his life and sank very low before getting sober. Even then, it took him years in recovery to develop his life skills to attain a modest level of productive, prosperous living. Barry's story is not unusual for people in recovery. Frankly, overcoming negative patterns is sometimes too much even for people in recovery, and relapse is common.

    I also quite recently read a book by Angela Duckworth called *Grit: The Power of Passion and Perseverance*. I enjoyed the discussion of the potential impact of talent versus grit, and the not-so-surprising conclusion that grit often leads to greater life success than innate talent. Though I understand that Duckworth was focusing on the impact of the characteristics of grit, she nevertheless casually discounted opportunity and luck, that is, life circumstances. Her examples, of West Point or Julliard-bound students, top-school grads vying for McKinsey employee placement, and Olympic athletes left me a bit sad for those of us unlikely to ever be presented with a chance to demonstrate either the grit or the talent required in such elevated circles, due to significant challenges stemming from those so-unconcernedly dismissed circumstances.

For kids growing up in oppressive cultures or environments that place little value on reason and logic, and that may focus on and reinforce attitudes of victimization and alienation, making good choices and taking right action can be difficult. In *Hillbilly Elegy*, Vance shared that joining the military and then subsequently pursuing higher education became his ticket out of the hillbilly culture rut. He felt lucky to break the cycle and escape the mire of his dysfunctional family and culture. But it is safe to say that many from such disadvantaged groups do not escape. They stay impoverished and discontented.

Vance mentions in his introduction that working-class whites, particularly along the Appalachian belt, are among the most pessimistic of groups with high incidence of unemployment, of drug addiction or alcoholism and of domestic or other violence. While churches are abundant in these communities, sermons and religious sentiments are "heavy on emotional rhetoric." Vance's account demonstrated that the churches were not offering much practical or social guidance to help congregants change these dismal patterns. In fact, some religious groups reinforced attitudes of mistrust of institutions, devaluation of education, and misguided compassion and tolerance for abusive behaviors.

For me, despite my regular church attendance as a child, my reasonably high intelligence, and completion of multiple college degrees, I nevertheless made bad choices and failed to capitalize on my opportunities for many years. Though I often lamented my impoverished circumstances and wished for a better life, I took action again and again in my teens and twenties that undermined any possibility of that better life materializing. I now joke that *I* was the bad influence in my life.

At that time, when I thought about my future, I assumed I was not likely to achieve significant financial or social success. I was a poor kid. I was also a druggie. True, I was a poor kid who happened to get a scholarship to go to college, but only because I happened to get good grades. But I believed I was unlikely to do much of anything with my degree. Hence the waitressing, the drinking and using drugs, and the continued association with the lower companions. I had no reason to believe I would or could have substantial success in my life. Significant, reality-based success did not exist in my experience, nor was it presented to me as possible, or as a viable goal. I did complete college, and I did well in school, not because I believed it would lead me to success and achievement of my goals, but because it was easy for me, it was free and something to do. And, it was nice that however much I was struggling with drugs and turmoil in my personal life, at least I did *school* well.

My life circumstances and upbringing resulted in a belief that little could or would ever change for me, and certainly not that simply asking God for help would make any difference. But it did. For so many years, on my own, even while employed or at school, after spending the minimal time required completing work or school, I recklessly plunged off into the night, usually starting with bars, then dealers, and then God-knows-what. In my mind, I would convince myself that I was somehow defying a society that was rigged against me. But inside I was sad and disappointed in my life. And I was afraid to want, to hope for, a better life. I had no faith that I could change my future. I had no faith.

Duckworth defines a formula for achievement that goes:

Skill x Effort = Achievement

My version, including the additional factor of life opportunities and luck might instead be:

Circumstances x Skill x Effort = Achievement

Circumstances in this formula can be a positive or a negative factor.

Adding faith, the formula might look like:

Circumstances x Skills x Faith x Effort = Achievement

Cognitive Faith

For me, after going to a meeting of a 12-Step program and having asked for God's help as directed, however gracelessly, I did not, for an entire day, make the choice to drink or use drugs. Then, the next day I asked for God's help, and once again, I did not make the choice to drink or use drugs. And so on and so on. Then, having asked for God's help, I got a new job. Then, having asked for God's help, I applied for a better job. Then I prayed on it, and decided to seek out some higher certifications to pursue a better job. Then… And so on. Every day I asked for God's help and slowly, one day at a time, I built this quite lovely life I have today.

I want to share two more short stories. I have a friend named "Jill." She was one of ten kids. When I met her she was unsure if she had graduated from high school. She too was staying sober, back when I was also still quite new to sobriety. I recall, at one point Jill decided to check on the status of her high school graduation. Surprised that she had indeed graduated, she applied for college. Today she is a prominent therapist.

Another friend, "Abby," a hair stylist, dreamed of having her own salon. I recall sitting in a diner with her one evening doodling possible logos for her salon. After a few years of foundational sobriety Abby was able to launch that salon, fortified by faith and good footwork.

I love these stories and I know of many more cases of individuals with only modest initial prospects finding success, in careers, in family and romantic relationships and in achievement of countless other life goals. All through faith and positive efforts. Miraculous? Perhaps on a small scale.

Now, maybe you are already as successful and happy as you could ever hope to be. Or maybe you do not have an alcohol or drug problem, or harrowing upbringing to overcome. Perhaps you are simply looking for the internal strength to make small improvements in an otherwise satisfactory life. Or you may be struggling with an altogether different but equally life-threatening challenge. But for challenges big or small, God can shore you up. God can help you make better choices and lead you to better outcomes. God can provide the strength that on your own you may lack. God can be, in any of these cases, a source of empowering strength, and that, as they say, ain't nothin'!

Therapy versus Faith?

I spoke recently with "Sean," the twenty-something son of a friend. He shared candidly that he was in therapy and had been for most of his adult life. "My therapist says I need to focus on my therapy and healing inside and abstain from dating because I don't seem to find healthy relationships." I sensed he was trying to put a positive spin on his loneliness. Many of his statements in this particular conversation began with "my therapist," or "in therapy…"

I have no opposition to therapy and have spent brief periods of time in therapy myself, getting through rough patches in my life. I think therapy can be a safe place to identify the root causes of issues and neutralize the power of unhappy events or unhealthy patterns. I further recognize that serious mental or emotional disorders may require ongoing support and monitoring. Without going too deeply into this, according to a report published in *Newsweek* in February 2014, about 20 percent of adult Americans suffer in any given year from some degree of mental illness, and 4 percent suffer with serious mental issues that somehow impede their ability to perform day-to-day activities, while just 1 percent suffer with a psychotic mental disorder that may require hospitalization or long-term treatment and care. So, *many* people will have episodes of mild to moderate depression, anxiety, or other mental illness. Most people, however, even when experiencing an episode of mental unwellness, nevertheless manage to cope, work, have relationships, and carry on a normal life.

But I have seen cases among my friends and acquaintances where a person essentially lives their life in therapy and in a kind of misery, focusing endlessly on their unhappy past or problems. It is an easy trap to fall into. I don't think therapists *intentionally* keep their clients as long-term patients, but I do know that not every therapist pushes for real recovery, that is, a true and lasting improvement in coping skills, improved happiness, and release from the bonds of the past or unhealthy patterns.

I am a believer in recovery.

Elkhart Tolle speaks of being fully present in your life as you live it in the *Power of Now* (Namaste Publishing, 2004). I do appreciate the concept of being fully present and *living* your life. Tolle suggests that we become fully focused through deep meditation. Through deep meditation, we can release our past, our "pain body," as he calls it. For Tolle, though, we must stay out of the mind and maintain focus on the body. I suspect this methodology may work for some: this deep communing with your deep self and removal of thought or the mind from the process. I also agree that it is sometimes *our heads*, ever at work analyzing, remembering, and considering, that can keep us in the bonds of past pain and our unhealthy behaviors. This is why endless sessions of therapy can lead to endless re-experiencing of our personal misery.

But I believe there is an alternative for recovery from pain and the emotional bonds of suffering, unhealthiness, and destructive or self-sabotaging behavior. And that answer is God and faith. This is the third and final compelling reason for having faith. God can heal. Not spontaneous, miraculous overnight healing of cancer, but slow, real, and equally miraculous mending of our big and small brokenness that keeps us from joy or from reaching for our dreams.

Without disparaging his work with the therapist, I asked this young man if he had any spirituality to support the therapy work he was doing to heal from his childhood dysfunction. He looked at me with surprise, a surprise I have seen before: surprise at the suggestion that spirituality may be part of a solution to a smart person's troubles. "I'm not talking about religion," I clarified. "But you might find that prayer and faith can prove to be a powerful part of achieving significant healing and getting past the negativity of your past and on to a more fulfilling life."

Frankly, I am not sure this young man accepted what I said. In fact, some of the toughest introductions to Cognitive Faith I have faced have been with smart people who honestly do not consider God or faith to be an intelligent, viable answer to their questions about happiness and success in life. In fact, I think this young man, who at the start seemed to respect my education and career, suddenly came to view me as a curiosity. Certainly he saw the suggestion of using spirituality as a tool as unexpected.

I nevertheless like to challenge smart people to think about faith, particularly scientists. During the Age of Reason, progressive thinkers were confident in believing the world could and would be fully explained though scientific laws. Today, however, most advanced scientific minds agree that there is much that is now, and is likely to remain, inexplicable. A faith proposition that embraces every bit of scientific knowledge, current or future, and that offers the benefit of personal empowerment should have some appeal. With Cognitive Faith, scientists need not be put on the opposing side of a faith debate, as in days of old. Today, advanced thinkers might well accept that a cognitive variety of faith or spirituality may tie in nicely with scientific fact and perhaps with some scientific mysteries as well.

So, with scientists, agnostics, and atheists, I ask, "Why not?" Why not try faith? This is not saying, "Try out a religion." It is saying that, as an experiment, do the actions suggested. It is nothing difficult or embarrassing. In fact, you can do it without anyone knowing or seeing. If intransigence in religious zealots is unattractive, it is even less so in scientists or self-declared intellectuals. We should not disparage a proposition without giving it a respectable amount of diligent assessment.

I have a whip-smart friend named "Mellie." I've known her for twenty years. Throughout that time, she has experienced some significant ups and downs in life. She is witty and attractive, and, as mentioned, smart as can be. Blows doors off on Jeopardy episodes. But she has had no enduring romantic relationship: she struggles with finances and jobs, and suffers from bouts of sadness and depression, fearing she will continue to be alone and with limited funds as she ages. Of course, we have talked about steps she might take to see improvement in her life, what she might do to meet someone to date, career actions she might take. And, of course, because she is a friend, I have suggested faith and prayer. "Naw, that's not for me," she says dismissively. And I have to say: I just don't get it. She has a free, potential solution, or, if not a solution, a free action she can take, requiring very little time or energy, to achieve possible improvement in her situation, but her answer is: no, it's not for her. That response is called contempt prior to investigation.

Pascal's Wager

Blaise Pascal, a seventeenth-century Age of Reason philosopher, postulated that even without definitive evidence of God's existence or non-existence, one is better off hedging one's bets by adhering to religion. If wrong, and God does not exist, there is no downside or dire consequence. However, if God does exist, that is, the Christian God of Pascal's world, and one chooses to disbelieve and not adhere to the religious strictures, the downside is eternal damnation. This philosophical dilemma is known as Pascal's Wager (Pensées, point 233, Digital Edition, 2017 Gianluca Ruffini).

I concede that I cannot scientifically prove God's existence. Nor can I prove that faith produces statistically significant, life-improving results. Anecdotally, I can say that choosing to have faith in a divine power, which I call God, has seemingly improved my outcomes. The results of the life, career, relationship, and happiness I now have and have had over the past many years seem considerable, compared to the relatively minimal investment required by my ongoing choice to practice faith.

In the 1600s, Pascal was exploring the dilemma of deciding or choosing to abide by and accept Christian doctrines, and particularly those tenets that rational intellectuals of his time rejected. Somewhat unreasonably, Pascal repeatedly asked, "how can we know it is not so?" of such doubtful events as the resurrection, life after death, and Immaculate Conception (Pensées, points 222, 223).

My version of Pascal's Wager requires no such suspension of reason. I simply propose entertaining, if not accepting, a belief that some form of God *may* exist. And, to entertain, if not accept, that through faith you could receive the very real benefit of empowerment. Some might argue that believers are merely deluded into a feeling of empowerment by their faith. That, through the power of suggestion, they are biased by their belief, attributing positive outcomes to their faith. Perhaps. I think this would make an interesting study. Regardless of its source, and regardless of the absolute truth of the efficacy of faith, I can attest that *tangible* improvements have indeed occurred in many areas of my life, and that the improvement in my life was greatly accelerated when I found a comfortable version of faith that did not diminish or offend my intelligence. If the investment in faith is minimal and requires no intellectual compromise, and possible rewards are significant, placing a wager on faith, that is, exploring faith, seems worthwhile, even sensible, for any rational thinker.

Ironically, I have found that the people with the very most to gain, those that are deeply unhappy or fighting battles with significant personal problems or dysfunctions, are often the most resistant to trying faith. Happier, healthier people are often the most willing to explore ways to enhance their life through examination and consideration of faith. So, you might want to ask yourself where you stand in this. Are you unhappy and resistant? Are you hoping for answers from therapy or other self-help? Do you find the idea of adding

Cognitive Faith

faith—as you have been taught faith—to your toolkit to be old-fashioned, contrary, or even embarrassing? My suggestion for *you* is simply to explore Cognitive Faith. It is most certainly *not* your grandma's version of faith.

Part Three
God

The Nature of God

     God in Heaven. God inside you. God, the ruler of the universe. God Almighty. Nature as God. God as goodness. Jesus Christ as God. Allah, El, Buddha, Jehovah, Krishna, Mother Earth. I heard one person say that God is Good Orderly Direction. You might hear any of these descriptors when you ask people about their God and faith. In general, I feel that whatever works for a person as a definition of God is fine. I certainly do not purport to offer much more than my own opinion, though I am, as already shared, uncomfortable with zealotry and any person's or religion's insistence that a particular definition represents *the only* truth about God, or condemns those that believe otherwise.

Cognitive Faith

In the earliest years of my recovery, in addressing or describing God, I borrowed from my Protestant Christian upbringing. I even attended church for a time. Very soon, though, I grew uncomfortable doing so. I again struggled with listening to the fantastical stories and moral admonitions. Whenever I interacted with the congregants, I felt like a poser. Further, when praying, I kept envisioning some white-bearded old fellow sitting on high, directing the activities of humans and answering their prayers. I found myself disbelieving my own view of God.

Then for a time, I resisted any defined God at all and adopted what I jokingly called a Star Wars faith. I "prayed" to the universe, which I thought of and described as tapping into "The Force." I defined The Force as a universal energy or strength that would empower or move a person toward goodness or positive existence. And, having spent quite a few years in a shadowy, unsavory lifestyle, I also, back then, talked about and believed in the existence of an equally powerful "Dark Side." The Star Wars films were such a cultural phenomenon during my adolescence and early adulthood that their lore had become iconic. My Star Wars version of faith offered me a way to speak about my beliefs without using words like God. And, somewhat embarrassingly, I liked that the Star Wars terminology, however tenuously, tapped into my inner science nerd.

At that time, I also enjoyed the flippancy of sharing my Star Wars faith with people. Looking back, however, I recognize that the levity and pop culture nature of my attitude toward my faith was actually a symptom of a flaw in my spirituality. At the time, I was not taking my faith very seriously, and, in recovery, this can be dangerous. Based on how my personal and business life was going, I could see that I was not on firm spiritual ground.

Still, though brief, my Star-Wars-faith era was a turning point for me. The Star Wars framing allowed me to embrace spirituality apart from my former Christian religion but without association with other equally problematic religions or quasi-religions. It was my first pass at defining my own faith, notwithstanding its commercial origins. Star Wars faith was a start for me, but as I wanted more from life—more success, more happiness—I required more substantial faith.

Over the subsequent years, I quietly and more seriously explored my understanding of faith and God. I very much liked the concept in Star Wars of there being a Force, rather than a God. Mainly because I was still uncomfortable with the term God and disliked the tendency to personify when using the word God. Once I abandoned the Star Wars terminology, for a number of years I used euphemistic phrasing like "universal energy," "divine power," "the infinite and unknowable life-force," and such. Frankly, however, that phrasing made me feel like a New-Age hipster, exactly the opposite of the *intelligent* spiritual person I wanted to represent. I began using the word God in later years but often quickly added the qualifying phrases, such as divine force and universal energy—and still do occasionally. But most often I

Cognitive Faith

simply say God and have made my peace with all the various associations that people have with the term. I know, in using the word God, or prayer for that matter, people have occasionally mistaken me for a *religious* person. Sometimes I correct them. Sometimes I do not. As I said, I have made my peace with God as the center of my faith. But, as this book shows, I still want to qualify what that means for me.

More important than the words I use is my final comfort with and belief in God, and thoughtfully formed ideas about what God is and is not. God is the architectural force that created the universe. All that is inexplicable in the universe— and there is yet much that is unknown— is God's domain. When I consider the vast, even miraculous complexity of the universe, the beauty of the world, life's existence, evolution, and the amazing path life has taken here—and potentially in other worlds or universes yet unknown—that is God's handiwork. Man has and continues to uncover divine, even miraculous, laws and order in nature and the universe through evolving sentience and the ability to study and discover. Cognitive Faith argues that these discoveries confirm and provide *evidence or proof* of God. I suspect that, as science continues to evolve, we will see and come to comprehend further order in areas that at present seem mysterious or even conflicting. As Einstein famously said, God does not play dice with the universe, and I also see it as doubtful that truly haphazard or contradictory laws are at work. Humans may never fully understand all that God has arranged, but my thought is that whatever more we uncover will engender principles that will continue to inspire human wonder.

God and Intention

But did God *intend* to have this world and universe become as it is now? Does God have a plan? This is where I believe many people still think much like our cave-dwelling brethren. They so want to understand God. To see God as through human eyes. To put a human face on God, and attribute human emotions or ideas to God. I do not believe that God has a human face or a human mind. This is akin to attributing to God a race or language. It is ethnocentric. I hold no belief whatsoever in a personified God. God is not a being, at least not in a form that resembles a human or has human goals or concerns. Attributing human form or intentions to God is once again an anthropomorphic error.

Many religions, current or ancient, represent God with human images, prophets, or humanistic deities. Jesus, Buddha, Mohammad, Krishna, angels. They give God a face and human feelings and purpose. But this is a most unlikely view. If, in the vastness of the universe, there is another life form, does that life form have a different God that closely mirrors their form and culture? Is it really likely that billions of years ago this humanistic God created this entire universe, then after a few billion years created Earth, then sat by for millions of years more waiting for man to evolve into a sentient but deeply flawed being who we can truly believe is

God's image? God *must* exist on a plane far beyond human morphology and intention.

If you want or need a visual metaphor, think of it this way. Get near a power-plant generator that is humming along, putting out millions of megawatts of power. You can *feel* that significant power is there. You cannot see it, but most certainly it is there, and you know that power can be directed to do amazing things. God is like that. I shy away from a visual definition of God, because doing so inevitably points up the limits of human comprehension, including my own. But the power of God is inherent in all that is, neither apart from matter nor distinctly matter itself. Instead, God is in, around and of our universe and beyond, and is the force, source, and energy that shaped and continues to shape our universe. Furthermore, God's power is omnipresent and ever ready to be accessed.

God as a Source of Power

God, though without a distinct form or face, is nevertheless available to each of us in a very individual, personal way, as an infinite source of power, energy, and strength. But God is not an ATM, a spontaneous healer of ailments, or a talisman that can prevent natural disaster or accidents. This is not to unequivocally say such things have never happened as a result of prayer or faith, nor to preclude the possibility that seemingly miraculous events could occur in the future. My opinion is that events which seem to be miracles are more likely just unusually good luck, on the extreme edge of statistical possibility, but apparently still possible, and not personally ordained by God.

    In general, we should not approach faith or God with an expectation of or hope for instant fulfillment of wishes, as though God were some genie from a bottle, or with an expectation that one can avoid all personal misfortune through God. Such thinking is not grounded in reality. Sorry to say, most of us are unlikely to become Jedi masters able to command the power of The Force to bend reality to our righteous will.

    I suppose it is human nature to desire big results and be swayed by propositions where big results might be offered. You need only watch late-night television to witness the wide variety of offers that will result in amazing weight loss or instant virility. I have read many self-help books and always bristle when the authors imply that all you must do is X, then you will have everything you desire. Three books come to mind.

    Most recently, I completed the book *You are a Badass*, by Jen Sincero (Running Press, 2013). Sincero uses example after example of her own success to indicate how easily anyone can just make up their mind about what they want and then go get it! If you do you are a badass; if you don't, you suck. I wondered throughout this book if Sincero had any real personal experience with adversity and overcoming challenges in her life. Apparently, she wants us all to quit our day jobs and pursue our dreams, get out of bed if we are depressed, and manifest what we desire. You know, just go buy an expensive car to demonstrate we are going to have financial success. Whatever.

In *The Secret* by Rhonda Byrne (Atria Books, 2006), a best-selling book with significant popularity in the mid-oughts, the author proposed that through "laws of attraction" and positive thoughts, individuals might have *whatsoever* they desired in their life. After several "true accounts" of fabulous, and I mean fabulous, wealth achieved, or healing of terminal, and I mean terminal, illness achieved, and other such wonders, I admit I did not even finish reading the book.

Then, in *Breaking the Habit of Being Yourself*, Dr. Joe Dispenza (Hay House, 2012) offered a more scientific and reasonable basis to a similar premise, to which we will return. His methodology of realizing dreams of wealth, health, or happiness was through a reprogramming of your brain, your cells, and your electro-chemical wiring, ultimately altering the very genes of your body.

Despite my cynicism about the promised incredible results, all these books had some propositions I embrace. I do believe that we need to take personal responsibility for our lives and that we can improve our outcomes by changing our thoughts and behaviors. But I find their need to offer success of the miraculous variety unsound. After reading these types of books, I find myself wondering about average people who try to meticulously adopt their advice, as I am sure many have. What if they do not receive the miracles? Then what? Books—or religions—that present their self-help or spiritual propositions in such a manner feel like faith-healing, snake oil, wonder cures, or get-rich-quick schemes. If you are not healed, then you must not have enough faith. If you do not attain fabulous wealth, then you did not do the process correctly and probably need to attend another costly seminar. Echoes of Scientology come to mind, with its pay as you go, and theoretically grow, courses.

I suspect the majority of people who enroll in coaching or attend seminars with these authors are not today among the fabulously wealthy, perfectly happy, or illness-free. I suppose that authors sell more books and seminars if tremendous wealth, astonishing healing, or other wonders are in the offing. But I think there are plenty of, perhaps more, people who are more sensibly looking for guidance and spirituality, with an objective of peace and comfort, and perhaps sustainable improvement, over unlikely and outlandish promises of spontaneous wealth and magical results.

As for God, I personally have no confidence in suggestions that God will deliver extravagant magical results through faith. I am deeply suspicious of big religious personalities with their big churches and their big promises. I do not believe that any version of spirituality can legitimately offer miraculous results. When presenting the truth or collecting evidence on the possible benefits of spiritual beliefs, with isolated exceptions of individual luck or good fortune, the more likely promise would be for simple and sustainable improvements in life circumstances, happiness, and serenity. In other words, a good life.

God does not Define Good or Evil

And speaking of good, in exploring and defining Cognitive Faith, I struggled with the concept of good and evil. I shared earlier that I did at one point firmly believe that a force for evil—the Dark Side in Star Wars lingo; the devil in Christian lingo—existed. I believed then that there were tangible forces that might on one hand pull a person toward light and goodness, or conversely toward darkness and dissolution. But as I reflected on the world, spirituality, and the complexity of human psychology, I came to a different and controversial conclusion.

I think that *God* is a force for neither good nor evil. This is a hard concept for most believers in religion. Most religions are based on dichotomies of good and evil, right and wrong, saved and damned. In Cognitive Faith, God is simply a source of power, energy, and strength. It is humans who create the good or the evil characteristics. Indeed, in our world *only* humans ascribe events and actions to be good or bad. In nature, killing is survival and not a moral issue. While animals may experience emotions, including fear, anxiety, sadness over loss, attachment akin to love, and perhaps contentment and a form of joy, it is humans alone who fret over what is right or wrong.

So, I no longer believe in the existence of a counterforce to God such as the devil or the Dark Side. Goodness and evil are human constructs, and they vary from culture to culture, with few, if any, absolutes. Even killing or torture can be accepted in many human ideologies if they serve to advance a culture's agenda, to defend others, or, occasionally to achieve a greater good. It is entirely possible for persons from two warring societies to each view, quite rightly, that their foes are evil and wrong, and to pray to their God for their opponent's defeat. Which side would you have God take in this case?

That said, I recognize that serious pathologies and abhorrent behaviors exist among humans. God is not, however, the arbiter of human right and wrong. Religions of all varieties, and governments too, have attempted to create the ultimate list of right and wrong, but to no definitive end. Of course, societal rules and laws, however imperfect, are imperative as a behavioral code for human populations. Still, a wide disparity exists between the various religions' and societies' ideas of moral rightness and wrongness. But such judgment is the purview of man, not God.

So, once again we have a good news / bad news scenario. If you were hoping that those evil-doers would get their comeuppance from God by burning in hell after death, or by coming back in another life as a cockroach, through bad karma or bad luck in this life, you may be disappointed. Instead, God is available to all. I repeat, God's power is available to all. There is no threshold of particular faith or good behavior or acts of spirituality that qualify you for God's power. Anyone can tap into it. It is the person who will channel to what purpose God's power is used.

Evil in the World and Morality

Having clearly asserted that good and evil are not the purview or the creation of God, I do not deny that good or evil behavior exists. Of course, goodness or evil have been historically defined within the tenets of a culture's religion and attributed to God's decree. As such, and as discussed at length earlier, a dominant religion's doctrines often underpin a culture's governance, laws, and beliefs regarding right or wrong, good or bad, moral or immoral behavior, and what is legal or illegal. Human understanding of good and evil, then, is often inextricably associated with religion and God, so it is helpful in understanding Cognitive Faith to explore these concepts.

Why is it that evil people succeed? Murderers, abusers, cheaters, haters. People are baffled, and rightly so, by the seeming success of so many people and agendas that are malevolent. It is true that some evil-doers have long and successful careers of doing wicked deeds. Some are able to spread vile hatefulness and enlist others into widespread or even global villainy, sometimes with absolute impunity. Worse, they may garner rewards such as power or wealth through their misdeeds. How can such "evil" succeed?

Here I return to the concept of right and wrong not being a God issue. Evil people are simply committed to their odious ideas, pathologies and agendas. They have clarity of focus. They work at it. Good people, when similarly committed to their good works, as frequently succeed. The truth is that a great percentage of people do not have such focus for either good or evil. Historically, we can pull only a few names out from the record books of those notoriously evil: Hitler, Stalin, Genghis Khan, perhaps a few of our more infamous serial killers, etc. Likewise, we can only pull a selected few that we consider famously righteous: Gandhi, Lincoln, Mother Theresa, etc. What we know about them is that in each case they were, or became at some point in their lives, dedicated to their respective intentions. Good or evil, however, became their focus, but was not something absolute, innate, or pre-ordained. Nor can we say that their ultimate goodness or evil was who and what they were for their entire lives. No, they lived lives that offered them, like any of us, choices. At some juncture, they turned, were drawn to, or were pushed toward a hateful or a virtuous choice. Then, again and again. Momentum reinforced the continuation in the direction of evil or good deeds, respectively, until they became a habitual choice. God did not create their evil or their virtues, nor is it for God to judge them.

I know this is deeply disappointing to those who wish for God to take a stand or have final responsibility for judging and punishing our human failings. It is just highly unlikely that such subjective decision-making can be assigned as God's responsibility. The real responsibility is man's, that is, human society's. We create understanding of good or right behavior through societal rules and laws that support good or virtue as best we can identify them. Often those rules or laws are deeply influenced by the culture's dominant religion, and in more recent times by societal special-interest groups, assorted religious groups among them. We must recognize and acknowledge the imperfect nature of the process, however. There will never be a single universal definition of right. And even within the parameters of largely acknowledged right, there will be moral paradoxes, loopholes, and contradicting opinions. At any given point in time, but especially in recent times, multiple conflicting stances or standards are vying for backing and ascendency. The sometimes-monumental shifts we see in what is considered right or wrong demonstrate that the definitions are indeed of man's making.

What is the alternative proposition? That God intentionally created a world where humans would be presented with good and bad behavioral choices so that God could then judge us? That God *intended* to have evil options presented to us and then uses a sliding scale to tally up the good and bad markers from our lives to ultimately judge and potentially punish us? And if so, whose rules are being applied by God? Christian rules? If so, which sect of Christianity? Muslim rules? Jewish? Hindu? Different rules for different people? Such divine judgment once again assumes

God to have an extraordinary concern about our behavior, presenting these evil or immoral choices in a game of temptation. This seems most unlikely.

    We can say with confidence though, that regardless of the source of the good or evil behavioral choices, making the choice is an individual one. Each person is confronted with a variety of choices throughout their lives, and each person chooses which path they will take, over and over. The understanding of the rightness or wrongness of the options is uniquely shaped for each person as well. Religion and culture are often at the center of this learning, and, in more recent years, schools, societal laws, and governmental dictates have also been influential. Finally, and most recently, media, including—in chronological order—books, periodicals, film, radio, television, the Internet, and social media, have all become shapers of human perspectives on morality. Still, each person interprets and adopts codes of right and wrong in individual and diverse ways.

    In discussing morality, Lawrence Kohlberg's hierarchy of moral development is often referenced. Kohlberg, a prominent American psychologist, spent much of his career during the 1950s categorizing levels of human morality. He suggests that the lowest level of moral development is based on avoidance of punishment and self-interest. This is also referred to as pre-conventional morality, because a person's morality at this level does not consider the impact of one's actions on others. Mid-level morality, which is based on conformity to rules and maintaining social order, is known as conventional morality. At the highest level, morality is based on so-called higher or universal principles and is referred to as post-conventional. The model presents morality as a progression through stages, assuming lower stages to be less evolved and higher stages superior. In Kohlberg's model, we all begin as children in the pre-conventional stages and mature into the conventional. Only a small percentage ever elevate morally to the desirable post-conventional stages (see Fig. 5)

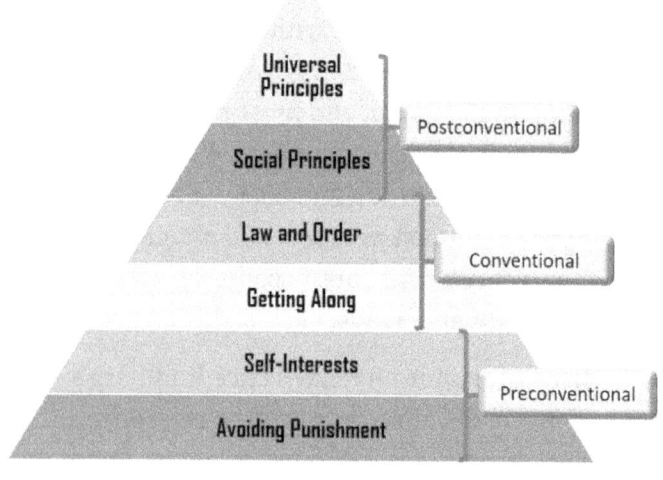

Fig. 5

Underlying this morality model is an assumption that self-interest and avoidance of punishment or pain are an inferior or deficient morality. It also assumes that society is able to define conventions that are generally good. Finally, Kohlberg suggests that there exists a divine, universally right morality that might be adhered to if one can elevate to that stage. As mentioned earlier, to date no religion or society has yet identified a universal set of principles that might act as the final word on morality. Scriptures vary widely and sometimes offer questionable or archaic prescriptions. Furthermore, many cultures have laws, societal conventions, religious tenets, or even popular pastimes that have demanded behaviors that challenge moral sensibilities. On a large scale, think of the Inquisition, or, as discussed below, the German population under Nazi rule. Or on a smaller scale, the hateful activities of the Ku Klux Klan, Al-Qaeda, or the IRA. Cognitive Faith stresses the idea that religions in particular, and society in general, may sometimes veer dramatically afield of good, sound morality.

    I recently finished reading a book called *KL: A History of the Nazi Concentration Camps* by Nikolaus Washsmann (Abacus Publishing, 2001). I was interested to see if the book shed light on how the general German population dealt with the shifting tides of ethical belief systems and conduct before and during World War II, in relation to internment, mass executions, and, later, extermination efforts. Of course, context is everything, and perhaps there is a reasonable allowance for all the millions of Germans who passively accepted the atrocities perpetrated over the many years of Nazi rule. For many, the question must have boiled down to self-interest. It would be hard to make an argument that simply because the Nazi regime presented internment and later systematic killing as an accepted societal decree most of the reasonable people of Germany accepted and aligned their actual morals with those dictates. Certainly, some did. But can those who adjusted their ethical belief system to conform to such an odious rule of law be seen as on a higher ethical plane than those who accepted or tolerated the situation for self-preservation?

Kohlberg's idea that there is a linear progression or a hierarchy of ethical goodness does not bear up under situations fraught with such challenges. Ethical beliefs, morality, and right behavior are individual in nature and situational. Individuals make countless choices over a lifetime, and these are not unilinear. Morality and ethical beliefs are sensitive to changes in environmental conditions, new information, and circumstantial personal choice. Surely even the most focused evil-doers, or, for that matter, focused do-gooders, had points in or parts of their lives where they were not so committed to their respective evil or good.

Given that few people, if any, are entirely evil or good, at what point should God begin to withhold power? Though not logical, many people prefer to believe that God can and should judge and withhold power from bad people and offer power and success exclusively to the good. The concept of God's power being universally available is an affront to those people who prefer religion's exclusive-club status. In most religions, as discussed earlier, adherents are righteous and saved, and non-adherents immoral and damned. Again, this is an unsound argument. If only a given religion's adherents are saved and good, which religion's principles is God applying?

And, how can these people explain the apparent success and abundance of the damned?

Unhealthy Behavior

What of unhealthy behavior? Why do so many people struggle with choices that involve behaviors that are clearly unhealthy? First, let's establish that unhealthy behavior is not generally a moral issue, as discussed above. Unhealthy behavior is usually not about right or wrong, though occasionally there is some overlap, for example, when a person's unhealthy behavior leads to illegal acts or when it harms or endangers others. Or, in some cases, when a religious group categorizes an unhealthy behavior as immoral, as in vices such as gluttony, lust, greed, etc.

Among unhealthy behaviors are a wide range of behaviors that plague people today, including but not limited to drug and alcohol abuse, eating disorders, relationship dysfunctions, career and financial mismanagement issues, smoking, unhealthy eating, obesity, self-mutilation, addictive gambling, and sexual excesses, to name just a few. I differentiate these unhealthy behaviors from deeper psychiatric issues, whose manifestations may fall outside the realm of apparent personal control, though I do believe that some lesser disorders, particularly anxiety disorders and compulsive behaviors, can be improved through self-management efforts and by recovery-focused faith. Understand that I am not implying that every person who occasionally indulges in an alcoholic beverage or who enjoys a friendly game of poker has a problem.

    Still, unhealthy or excessive versions of these behaviors are quite prevalent and may wreak havoc in the lives of those partaking in the behaviors. They impact the lives of their loved ones and can impact our social systems as well. Why, then, do people do these things?

    Like evil behavior, discussed above, sometimes being the unhealthy kind of "bad" is easier than being the healthy "good." Partaking excessively of alcohol, drugs, or even tobacco or food, can sometimes provide temporary relief from environmental stressors, mitigate feelings of awkwardness or social anxiety, calm frustrated desires for love or acceptance, or ease unpleasant thoughts of painful past or present circumstances. Or they can simply provide passing pleasure. It can be satisfying to eat a large, calorie-excessive meal. It can be gratifying to spend money on that eighty-seventh pair of shoes or another expensive electronic toy. Hooking up with that bad boy in a bar or that sexy coworker outside your marriage may momentarily make you feel more desirable or less lonely. The downside of these behaviors may not be clear immediately, but in many cases in the long term they lead to additional unhappiness or undesired outcomes.

    If these words seem harsh or judgmental, please remember I have an extensive personal history of unhealthy behavior, including drug and alcohol abuse, smoking, sexual misconduct, and dishonesty. This book is about faith, tapping into the power of faith, for personal improvement and peace. But if a person behaves badly, or unhealthily, that is not the fault of faith.

Some people do not like the idea of being accountable for their lives and actions. They want to blame their unhealthy behavior on society, circumstances, or the influence of others. It is true that some people have significant, dreadful circumstances, past or present, which drive them from a psychological perspective to adopt the unhealthy behaviors. Others, seeing the apparent ease in the lives of others, either in their world or in the celebrity-studded media, may simply feel entitled to quick wealth, personal luxury, or passing pleasure, and resent that opportunities, riches or indulgences are not easily available to them. They then justify their bad behavior, small or large. From the distressingly common petty gaming of the system to high crimes, far too many people choose to disregard legal, societal, or even religious moral principles, and are affronted at negative consequences when they arise.

I am a believer in personal accountability. You can only change behavior that you own as *your* behavior, *your* choice. Taking personal responsibility for your actions is not easy, but until you accept that you are responsible, you are a victim. While playing the role of victim, there is little opportunity for making changes or improvements in your behavior. But if, at some point, you want something different, something better, *you* have to start doing different things.

Cognitive Faith

Faith can be a start, but as it has been said "faith without works is dead." Uniquely for humans, at least uniquely on earth, free will is indeed at work.

I read an interesting article online by a woman named Michele Carter titled "Abiding Loneliness: An Existential Perspective" (PhilosophicalSociety.com, 2003), in which the writer explores the manifestation of loneliness among humans and the relationships between this experienced emotional state and existential philosophy. Existentialism, as a philosophy and sometimes a therapeutic perspective, highlights the isolation that every person faces of individual consciousness apart from, and independent of, other human beings. However, in this apartness, this loneliness, we are confronted, says Carter, "…with two of life's most important questions: What is life really all about, and how should I use my freedom to define myself? The line about God "being dead" [as Nietzsche said] is another way of saying that all the pressure and responsibility for leading a meaningful life lie squarely on *our* shoulders. We, not God, decide what we become. We and we alone are the authors and governors of our moral life." In existential philosophy, according to Carter, God's existence is not denied, but free will and personal responsibility are foremost.

This ability to define and choose moral behavior is what sets humans part from other animals. In nature animals follow instincts alone. Choice is very limited. But, as humans, all day, every day we are offered the opportunities that come with making personal, individual choices. The decisions that lead to wickedness or to unhealthy behavior boil down to free will; we *can* choose to be better. Which leads to a discussion of goodness.

Goodness

If God doesn't care, and there is no cosmic consequence for bad behavior, why bother to be good? Religions at least offer a reward for good behavior. If you are good you will…go to heaven. You will…be reincarnated as a more advanced or higher-caste being. You will…have good karma. This reward/punishment and tally-sheet morality is, as already discussed at length, deeply flawed and requires blind acceptance of some defined set of tenets, which may or may not fully address life's challenges or satisfy intelligent reasoning.

If instead, God's power is available to all without judgment, here I want to encourage you to access that power for good. Make a choice now. Pray for God's help to live your life in goodness. God's power will follow, as promised, in the direction you choose. So, choose goodness. There will be moral dilemmas; you will have to make choices that might challenge your ideas. There will be evil, wrong-doing, and hurtfulness around you. Pray for God's help to guide you to refrain from such activity yourself. You are not wrong or morally flawed because you do not "stand up" at all times for good or right behavior. But pray to have kindness and goodness in your heart. Pray to have love and decency in your heart. Pray for God to help *you* be a good person.

When people ask me, "Why? Why should I be good?" all I can say is that being good has rewards. Not rewards in heaven or in a next incarnation, but right here. We know that bad or unhealthy behavior can lead to undesired outcomes. Having fear, hatefulness, negativity, and blame in your heart and thoughts moves you and creates a momentum that reinforces and perpetuates bad or unhealthy circumstances. I think again of the vicious cycles of self-defeating negativity Vance wrote of in *Hillbilly Elegy*.

The opposite is also true. Few people end up in jail from doing good. I have not had a single incident of physical violence in a relationship in over thirty years, though in the preceding years I experienced abuse and emotional mistreatment while living my unhealthy lifestyle. While ill health can befall anyone, some unhealthy behavior leads more surely to those ills. Good acts move you into the path of more good acts. Filling your heart with loving good feelings translates into actions that can bring more love and goodness to you.

It is not always easy to be or even to pray to be good, because sometimes being wicked or "bad" is easier and gratifies. Petty lies, thefts, cheating, meanness are easy to justify. Sometimes there are real or emotional rewards, sometimes the breaches provide self-gratification or self-interest, or stroke the ego. Sometimes, fear or other emotions drive you to behave wrongly or fail to adhere to your espoused good beliefs. But remember Newton's laws of motion. Ethical compromises can create momentum that can be hard to break, or may simply make further lapses easier.

 Still, perfectly moral behavior—post-conventional per Kohlberg—may be challenging even to define, let alone attain. Over the days and years of a life, a person may indeed compromise morality or goodness for self-interest or in accepting a clearly questionable group or societal morality, as in the case of German general population during the 1930s and through WWII. Such breaches, whether big or small, may impact a person's self-esteem or internal moral constitution. In Cognitive Faith, we suggest that people aim or pray for good or right behavior. And to recognize, that, in making choices, good or bad, we are establishing patterns in our life, patterns which may carry their own momentum and can become habit.

 The existence of religion among humans since the earliest ages of man, and religion's unfailing, if diverse, codification of morality, demonstrate that people do seem to need a moral compass. Without such codes, violent, hateful agendas, anarchy, or unbridled, self-serving behaviors might have prevailed, and civilization, especially on a larger scale, might have been impossible. In our current modern world, we see that moral lessons are taught through numerous and sometimes conflicting forums. Religion, schools, popular media, and laws, of course, have made morality a complex and far-flung subject, and the various sources often present conflicting principles. Pop culture in particular offers little foundation for moral or good behavior, often venerating the basest of human conduct. Furthermore, our legal system is deeply influenced by advocacy groups promoting their interests, interests that may have questionable or ill-conceived morality. The complexity of the world today and competing influences may make the good, right, or moral path difficult to decipher.

     Nevertheless, you need to believe that "being good" matters. Remarkably, despite the existence of and outspokenness of extreme hate and divisive factions, and many, many more subtle voices in our cultures and media engendering messages of discord and discontent, an encouraging number of us do have some sense of what being good means. Goodness is kind, not cruel. Goodness is loving, not hateful. Goodness is tolerant, not intolerant. Goodness is gracious, not antagonistic. Goodness is productive, not destructive. Goodness is caring and generous. Often, we know the good when we see it. We simply have to feel compelled to embrace choosing good over wrong, evil, or bad behavior.

     I challenge you to accept full responsibility for your actions. You do not have to be entirely good, but get out of the business of justifying bad behavior. There is no rationale for doing wrong. No one else is to blame; no one "made you" do wrong. You are always making choices. Take ownership. Stop playing the victim. If you have failed today to do the right behavior, own it, and perhaps, if possible, rectify it. Or try to do better next time. Certainly, accept it if undesirable consequences come from your actions.

Because over the years I have had regular interactions with people just beginning the recovery process after problems with drugs or alcohol, I have interacted with many people who do not want to accept consequences for their bad behavior. It is natural to wish for impunity when we stumble ethically. It is true that not every person suffers the same consequences. Nevertheless, lamenting the unpunished actions of others when presented with serious consequences for our own misdeeds does not justify resisting or discounting that the consequences were appropriate. Police sometimes say, "Don't do the crime if you don't want to do the time." Lawbreakers hope not to be caught, but, if caught, must accept their sentences and all the possible future consequences as well. Better to aim for preemptively good behavior.

I cannot know if I have convinced you to choose goodness over evil. I sometimes wish I could adopt the belief that certain and awful punishment awaits evil-doers after death or through karma. What I can say is this: When you live your life pursuing unpleasant, hurtful, or destructive ends, you are in essence creating an environment where unpleasant, hurtful, or destructive events and situations will manifest in your life. As such, there may be side effects, consequences, or outcomes that may not be positive or pleasant. And yours may not be a happy life.

Cognitive Faith

I cannot guarantee that being good will always result in happiness or in only good things coming to you in life. But when you focus on good, loving, productive living, you prime your brain to seek and make choices to achieve these goals. Add the power of faith to this worthy goal of upright living, and this is where God steps back into the equation.

Part Four
You

The Action of Prayer

Having faith or a belief in God does not in and of itself translate into improvement in one's life. Faith is not an action. To enlist and harness the potential power of faith, any kind of faith, requires action. In traditional religions, adherents may perform a number of actions in association with their faith. They may attend services in a church or a temple. They may read or study the Bible or Koran or some other sacred book. They may perform rituals such as blessings or special preparations of food. Yet, there are plenty of devoutly religious people who are unhappy or troubled, whether financially, in their romantic or personal lives, or with unhealthy addictions or behavioral patterns. So, clearly faith by itself is not particularly a remedy.

Prayer is another action often performed by people involved with formal religions as part of their observance. The act of focusing one's mind and reciting or thinking through prayerful words or thoughts expends energy, just as physically walking into a church or temple does. Prayer, in my estimation though, for very little investment of actual energy, offers the potential for vastly superior returns.

You may, having read to this point, agree with some of the propositions of Cognitive Faith. But up to this point Cognitive Faith has been presented as a point of view, not a set of actions. Here, we discuss the action of Cognitive Faith, in fact the only essential action, which is that you pray. While reconciling faith ideologies, particularly the belief in a divine power or God, and aligning faith with scientific fact are worthwhile, Cognitive Faith offers more. Indeed, Cognitive Faith offers an actionable path to achieve empowerment and improvement for you and your life circumstances. To see these positive outcomes, however, you must be willing to take targeted action. Too often, prayer occurs in a silo, only within the context of a religious service or narrowly prescribed ritual. This is particularly true for people who exercise their faith primarily by attending church or by participating in formal spiritual sacraments.

To illustrate, let's use attending religious services as an example. If you go to a service, the minister—priest, rabbi, or whoever—directs the content. Even the prayer that takes place within the service is prescribed. The nature or focus of the sermon or prayer, then, may or may not directly address your unique needs or desires. Setting aside earlier concerns about literal acceptance of religious lore, or about buying into a religion's behavioral and social doctrines, you are still spending your "faith time" being guided by the ideological or topical choices of that religious leader.

Having attended many services myself over the years, occasionally I have heard a sermon that was personally gratifying to me, that seemed to speak to my circumstances. But more often, the topics were not personal to me. They may have been interesting; they may even have been positive and good to have heard. But empower me through faith? In most cases, they did not. And, in a number of cases, I attended services which, in fact, had the exact opposite effect. Instead of lifting me up, the words of the sermon seemed to directly or indirectly judge me, to manipulate me, or to highlight the conflicts I had about religious doctrines. For me, I found that spending time participating in attending church services was not worthwhile.

Prayer Versus Meditation

Other spiritual programs encourage meditation as the preferred practice. Is meditation the same or as effective as prayer? The primary goal of meditation is to clear day-to-day mental clutter and counter-productive or taxing thoughts from the mind. The clearing away of thoughts is accomplished in various ways. The meditator may clear the mind by repeating chants over and over, by listening deeply to bells or music, by fixing attention on a flame or a point on the horizon, or through controlled breathing, exercise, or attention to the body instead of the mind. I believe that these activities are extremely calming and helpful. I have attended numerous retreats and spiritual events that included such practices. I personally enjoy them.

But meditation is not prayer. Prayer according to the Oxford English Dictionary is "a solemn request for help or expression of thanks addressed to God." It addresses God. It requires thought and requires the brain to be engaged, not turned off. And, importantly, in addressing God you can tap into the true power of prayer. In addressing God purposefully, your prayer can have focus and direction. I believe all prayer offers some benefit. So even sitting in a church and reciting a familiar rote prayer may bring about positive changes for you. The only difference, and it is a significant one, is that individual prayer is self-directed. When you intentionally engage with God, you can direct or control how God's power will be manifested. Purposeful prayer is the method, and because Cognitive Faith is disentangled from religious ritual, this prayer can be done anywhere and anytime.

Conscious Contact

Cognitive Faith encourages integration of prayer and "conscious contact" with God into all your daily activities. The phrase "conscious contact" is the parlance of people in recovery and reflects the need in recovery for spiritual support throughout daily activities, not just within, say, a meeting of Alcoholics Anonymous. To truly access the power that faith offers, Cognitive Faith suggests that you reach out to God as often as you can, that you develop a habit of drawing the power of your faith into your daily life. You can pray about all parts of your life, big and small. The potential returns are great, because prayer costs nothing, can be done anywhere, and can be focused individually to your specific needs. The prayer is also delivered when you might most need God's support.

So, in speaking to God, include some indicator of the help, the movement, or the direction that you would like God's power to give or take you. For example, early in my sobriety, my prayer was: "God help me stay clean," or "God help me get through this event without drinking." You can send a shout-out to God when you open your eyes in the morning. There is no need to get on your knees or strike a lotus pose. Nothing wrong with either of those things, and I personally do occasionally sit quietly and do more formal prayer. But it works even if you do not do it formally. You can close your eyes to pray. Or not. If you pray or speak to God while you are driving, I suggest keeping your eyes open.

You can use any words you like for your prayers. For the most part, I speak to God conversationally. But I have also been known to incorporate wording from prayers I have seen in published books, and I even found a few passages from the Bible that I like. You can feel free to borrow phrasing from a former religious affiliation, or a current religious affiliation for that matter, or from other self-improvement processes you may have used. When tapping into the power of God, there is no specific prescription required. God accepts all languages and all forms of communication.

For me, with sobriety pretty well in hand after thirty-plus years clean and sober, my prayers these days include simple requests for guidance, gratitude for all the many good things in my life, and prayers for the well-being of others. But I still say prayers throughout my day, inviting God's support into all areas of my life. Going into a business meeting? "God, help me present myself well in this meeting." Feeling a little insecure in my relationship? "God, please fill me with understanding and help me be a loving partner." Unsure of what action to take? "God, direct my steps and help me make a good decision." Dealing with an unhealthy pattern? "God, help me change." Have a career or personal goal? "God, lead me toward this goal and help me achieve it."

It is perfectly okay to ask for the things or outcomes you want. In Cognitive Faith, there is no righteousness in a vow of poverty or a preference for humble living. It is okay to want and ask for financial or career success. It is okay to want to have your dreams fulfilled. But remember, God is not an ATM machine, nor a genie granting wishes. Prayerfully asking for God to empower you, to help you, simply directs God-power into the physics of your world. It is an action that impacts other actions. It creates momentum.

Once you put a desire or a request out to God though, you can't just sit waiting for a miracle to happen. You are still required to take action. In recent years, I have been working in corporate human resources, focusing on career training and development, and therefore I am often approached by people wanting to advance their careers. I always suggest doing traditional career footwork. For example, performing their current job with excellence, expanding their skill sets by volunteering for broader responsibilities, doing research for the types of positions or career avenues the person is interested in, sometimes enrolling in school or training programs, or, in some cases, updating their resume and applying for jobs. The usual stuff. Of course, because I work within a corporate setting, I cannot say, though I would really like to, "Do all those things and make sure to pray about it too." Prayer is the secret sauce. Prayer potentially puts divine guidance and energy around the career moves you make. The same advice applies in goals or desires of any kind. Apply the force of faith, God's power, then do whatever logical footwork is before you, and the action with be divinely directed.

As I mentioned above, prayer is an action and the action of prayer will begin the process of reaction. As you interact in the world, your behavior and presentation will be influenced by your prayers and by the God's energy. Repeated prayer, repeatedly focusing your thoughts toward your personal goals and desires, changes you. Think back to the Take Control model explained earlier. Your thoughts deeply impact your emotions and resulting behaviors. When

Cognitive Faith

you choose to generate prayerful thoughts focused on your positive goals or desires, you alter your future behavioral choices. You alter how you feel. This process may work when simply framed as an affirmation, but is accelerated when framed as prayer, drawing divine support.

In *Breaking the Habit of Being Yourself*, Dr. Dispenza indicates that he believes changing your thought patterns or habitual thoughts, literally alters your atomic or even sub-atomic make-up, and over time your very genes. As Dispenza phrases it, "Neurons that fire together, wire together." I cannot say how deeply into our biology our thoughts go, but I know that when we focus our minds on our goals we create neural pathways to that thought. Repeated thoughts or prayers reinforce those pathways. In going about your day-to-day life, you continually access data from your brain, including a vast repository of information from your life experiences and learning, and perhaps from some deep human instinctual wells of human gen or, as Carl Jung liked to call it, the collective unconscious.

While some of this access is conscious – you deciding to think about a specific thing – much data is accessed without conscious thought to direct our actions throughout our day. For example, we give very little thought to driving, though the task is complex and requires moment-to-moment action. More significantly, we rarely stop and map out exactly how we will respond to others, nor precisely what actions we will take for our entire day. Imagine if you did this. "I'm sorry Joe, can you wait a few minutes for my response? I need to think about it and write down some appropriate response points." Now, perhaps doing so might give us better interactions, but we humans instead, in most cases, plow forth and speak. While we call it talking off the top of our head, it might more accurately be called automated talking, pulling cues, learning, and reactions from the brain's deep reservoirs of behavioral response.

One of the very important lessons I learned as a recovering drug and alcohol abuser is that some of the deep-rooted response cues that habitually pop up for me, or did for much of my life, are self-defeating. I did not consciously *decide* to defensively argue with authority figures, nor did I *intend* to be immoral or unseemly in my social interactions. While drinking and using drugs, my behavior and my life careened in unintended directions, and the outcomes of events seemed hopelessly beyond my control. I blamed others, society, bad people, bad luck, my economic situation, and more when things went wrong, and, for a time in my life, lots of things went wrong. This is true for most extremely troubled people, but also, on a lesser scale, any person whose life is not as they would prefer. The difficulty may be only in one area or across all areas of life. But for each of us with dysfunctions, big or small, the root of the trouble may seem, and to some real extent may be, beyond the person's ability to consciously alter.

To successfully recover, people with deep unhealthy patterns must be willing to change their actions. This begins with attentively, willfully resisting the harmful pattern.

Cognitive Faith

However, such white-knuckle recovery cannot last, because ingrained patterns do indeed run deep, and soon enough automated responses will again resurface. To manage a lasting recovery or sustained improvement, we need to reprogram the deeper landscapes of our minds to create an alternate, healthier wellspring of responses and reactions. Over the years, these healthier patterns will become equally ingrained. But how? We cannot instantly change all the many large and small events or lessons of our lives that cumulated in the self-destructive, unhealthy, or self-defeating personality we now have. It takes time to create new, purposefully healthier input. The fortification, the enabling power that makes the change possible, comes through God and faith. Prayer and the regular application to God for support shores up the individual in bridging the developmental gap.

While Dr. Dispenza suggests that radical change can be achieved in a few weeks of focused practice, I am skeptical of that accelerated timeline. Nevertheless, I do think he was onto an important underlying truth about the relationship between our thinking, conscious thoughts, and programming on a more subconscious level. Dr. Dispenza stays in the realm of science and behavioral science, but his proposition of tapping into and shaping the underlying elemental "energy" we are made of seems to parallel Cognitive Faith's spiritual energy. In either case, individuals may take action to harness forces or energy to empower the changes they would most like to manifest.

In Cognitive Faith, prayer is the simple, powerful methodology. A reasonable question is whether positive self-talk would work as well as prayer. If the goal is simply to feed more positive fodder and suggestions into the well of our subconscious minds, why must God enter the equation at all? So, here let me say that I do believe that good self-talk and affirmations, meditation, and other therapeutic techniques are worthwhile. They are likely to move your behavior and life in a positive direction. I have spent many hours incorporating such practices into my recovery regimen. But earlier I called prayer and faith the secret sauce. And I meant it.

In programs for recovery from drug and alcohol abuse, belief in a higher power is considered essential. The reason is simple. Left on our own, most often our patterns will lead us back to drinking or using. Most of us have *years* of experience failing to manage our problem on our own. *Years* of trying to improve on our own and relapsing. We *must* tap into strength beyond our own. Some people who struggle with the concept of God or a higher power may struggle with recovery.

Here again, I want to stress that the overcoming of unhealthy or limiting patterns is not simply for deeply troubled people, such as addicts or alcoholics. The principles apply for any self-defeating or detrimental behaviors or habits that may be inhibiting a person from achieving their goals or personal fulfillment. Relationship and family happiness, health improvement, and career growth or satisfaction are all possible targets for faith-accelerated success.

The act of prayer, of turning one's mind to God and speaking, is a simple thing. Even if you do not believe in God or in prayer, it can work. As discussed in the Nature of God chapter, God is not a judging being. God does not have petty human emotions. You can put your desires into prayer, not believing for a minute that the prayer will have any impact, and it will still work. The action will still create a response and a reaction on a level that is more elemental than your skeptical thoughts.

Not a Zero-Sum Equation – It's Chaos

One more important distinction on cause and effect needs to be explored here. In an earlier section we described Newtonian laws of physics. Newton's laudable laws are indeed at work all around us. When you play a game of golf, you see Newton's perfect laws in action. You are grateful that a small miscalculation in the angle of your shot results in your ball traveling only a bit off course. We can accurately apply Newtonian laws to most sports, construction, air travel, gunfire, and driving.

On the other hand, a good many "systems" in our physical world do not play out mathematically by Newtonian rules. Such systems are said to be Chaos Systems. The main features of Chaos Systems are: 1) imprecision in predictability; and 2) sensitivity to small influences. We can see numerous Chaos Systems with our own eyes. The most familiar large-scale example of such a system in science is weather. No matter how much we know about weather, and we know quite a lot, we nevertheless cannot gauge or accurately predict weather. We also cannot understand how or why weather events have the exact outcomes they do, even in retrospect. Weather events very often defy our expectations or our best understanding of the contributing factors at work. Underlying chaos theory is a tested and confirmed acceptance that, in chaos systems, small variables, often unidentified, can and do result in substantial, sometimes enormous, differences in outcomes.

    This is in direct contradiction with the Newtonian law of equal forces, that is, the law indicating that a new force must be of equal power to change the initial situation. Smaller forces in Newtonian physics would have smaller impacts, and very small forces would have very little impact on an outcome.

    Earlier, we discussed that every person will inevitably face life challenges, events that will impact you and push your life in undesired directions. Some of those events are truly devastating: deaths, debilitating illnesses, failed relationships, career or financial setbacks, etc. I also mentioned that it is natural and unavoidable that those events will push you and your life in a particular direction based on the nature of the event. I also mentioned that, per

Cognitive Faith

Newtonian laws, your life may continue in that undesired direction unless or until a new force is applied.

So, if the world ran only on strict Newtonian physics, when negative events happen, a countering, positive force would have to be "equal and opposite" to fully counteract the negative event. If Newton's laws alone applied, a small action would only result in a small change. When confronting serious life challenges, that is, big negative events, or a lifetime of habitual negative patterns of behavior, it might seem useless to take action at all, because it would be impossible to initiate a sufficient or equal counter-force to push your life in a new direction. Indeed, many people do simply give up and become victims of circumstance. They fail to see any hope of personally effecting changes in their lives. They complain or despair, further enforcing and flowing with the negative forces at play. They might feel powerless, thinking their only hope is for some significant or even miraculous outside force to enter the equation and move them in a more favorable direction. I think here again of battered Patti with her patched eye and unhappy situation.

But importantly, *many* human systems *do not* play strictly by those Newtonian rules and instead integrate chaos-systems rules. Your health, illnesses, relationship and career paths, most behavior choices, and innumerable other human systems simply do not have a strict action-reaction "zero-sum" set of rules. The exact same behavior—applying for a job or smoking cigarettes—can have wildly different outcomes on a matched pair of individuals. Further, it is proven that small adjustments or seemingly inconsequential actions can lead to substantial changes in results. The specific outcome of a given human action can often not be accurately predicted, and effects can be significantly non-commensurate.

For example, we can say that submitting a job application is the path to getting a job. But some people are offered jobs without ever applying. Some apply for a hundred jobs and do not receive a single job offer. We can say that smoking cigarettes can lead to lung cancer. Yet, some heavy smokers do not develop cancer. The truth is that behaviors and changes in behaviors can, and often do, have unexpected or surprising outcomes.

Science suggests that underlying even the most inexplicable variations in the outcomes of chaos systems, patterns exist, on larger scales, and can be identified. However, this will not help you individually with predicting outcomes for your own actions on a day-to-day basis. Instead, we have to embrace the idiosyncratic nature of human life.

So, when it comes to responses to life's challenges, the variable nature of outcomes in human systems asserted by chaos theory offers some interesting possibilities. In *Breaking the Habit of Being Yourself*, Dr. Dispenza cites a study where one set of students were told to *think* about developing a specific skill, and the second set were instructed to actually practice the skill. Both sets of students, when tested later, exhibited similar levels of proficiency in the skill. I am not suggesting that any person wanting to effect a change, or responding to challenges in their life, not do any footwork. I am suggesting that the mental activity, such as prayer, *is* footwork. And according to the laws of chaos systems, it may indeed produce significant results disproportionate to the energy expended.

This is yet another of those good news / bad news scenarios. The good news is that you may be able to significantly change your future by doing actions that might not seem significant, such as prayer or minor footwork. The bad news is that even small actions taken that are not moving you in a desired direction, or are counterproductive, can also have significant impact. We have all seen cases of seemingly small life choices leading to or resulting in monumentally life-changing outcomes. A single instance of unprotected sex can result in lifetime of parenthood. A choice to try a drug or drink at a party can result in a devastating accident or trigger a quick descent into drug or alcohol addiction.

Two actual cases come to mind for me. "Vivian" was a woman I knew in my earliest years of recovery. She did not stay sober initially, which is not uncommon. However, though other people relapse with consequences only commensurate with or similar to their previous unhappiness, Vivian, in that brief revisiting of her former lifestyle, contracted HIV. In another case, "Hank," during his brief "slip," had a serious car accident that killed the other driver, and his next attempt at sobriety occurred in prison, where he was completing an eight-year sentence for second-degree murder. Actions taken with impunity dozens of times may at any single point carry a lifetime of consequences.

Though cause and effect are at work in human systems, the relationships between factors are tremendously variable. The best advice is to pray for the outcomes you desire, take responsible action, and accept the outcomes.

If the word *pray* is objectionable to you, don't call it prayer. Call it meditation, affirmations, or even self-talk. If you object to the word *God*, call it another term you find acceptable. I have several agnostic friends who comfortably tap into the universal force by such semantic adjustments. God does not mind. Frankly, their interpretation of spirituality and prayer may be considered as accurate as mine. If you have read earlier chapters, you have seen that I too have grappled with the religious associations of these words.

Still, after numerous semantic gyrations, I have settled on the simple words faith, prayer, and God, even knowing the words bring up troublesome associations for some. I want and need my beliefs, my faith, to be bigger and infinitely more powerful than me. I feel that the vastness and complexity of the known universe warrant words with divine associations. For whatever time I have here on this planet, I choose to commune with and seek energy from this infinite power, which I call God. But it can be different for you. One of the beauties of Cognitive Faith is that it does not judge the nature of any person's practice of faith. The only rule, and really it is my rule, is that you pray without judging, condemning, or harming others.

In the end, the action of faith is so simple. Just say a prayer. You can do it right now. You can say whatever prayer you know. Or simply speak to God with no prayer structure at all. Doing this, saying a prayer or sending a specific thought to God, *is an action*. It will create movement, per Newtonian physics. In your mind, electro-chemical activity will take place. It will have an impact on your further thinking, your emotions, and your behavior. It can, as promised at the outset of this book, produce tangible and sustainable improvements for you.

I mentioned earlier in this section that, these days, I include wishes for the well-being of others in my prayers. While there seems to be a clear relationship between consciously praying for one's own personal improvement or well-being and experiencing personal improvement, praying for others may be less clear. In fact, rationalists may even argue, as discussed above, that the prayer we do to fortify our own lives may equate to positive self-talk, and the outcomes are the natural result of improvement in one's mental state and improved subsequent behavior. But can praying for others have a tangible impact? In cases where the prayed-for person is in direct contact with the person doing the praying, perhaps a positive influence may be exerted due to improved responses or other behavior when interacting with the subject. But what of prayer for far-removed, unknown, or people you might have minimal interaction with? Can your prayer impact them?

In *Breaking the Habit of Being Yourself*, Dr. Dispenza cites a study of intercessory prayer for blood-infection patients done in 2000. The patients that were prayed for purportedly had improved outcomes. As a twist, though, the patients being prayed for were ill *a decade earlier.* Despite the timing discrepancy, the prayed-for patients still experienced improved outcomes over non-prayed for patients. Dispenza's well-intended point relates to the potential power of our thoughts and prayers to influence outcomes within the fluid and somewhat little-understood space-time continuum. In researching, I must admit I found little scientific evidence of studies that demonstrated the efficacy of any intercessory prayer. Leonard Leibovici, who conducted the study mentioned above, admits that his study was done somewhat light-heartedly was intended to demonstrate that prayer offers comfort and help, but was not a controlled trial.

Are prayers for others a waste of time then? I still think not. In every case of intercessory-prayer research I found, those performing the prayers were not related to the subjects. I suspect the outcomes might be somewhat more significant if a study was conducted with persons praying for those they love or care about deeply, that is to say, those they are "entangled with."

In quantum science, two widely separated but "entangled" particles can react simultaneously to a stimulus or influence on *just one* of the particles. Imagine it. One particle is exposed to a positive or negative influence, and the other particle, miles or light years away, with no physical connection, reacts as if also experiencing the positive or negative influence. This was referred to by Einstein as "spooky action," and Einstein was troubled by the evidence of such a relationship between particles, feeling that some explanation or a logical causal factor was lacking. In fact, this entanglement has been repeatedly demonstrated scientifically ("Entanglement" by Devin Powell, *Discovery Magazine*, July/Aug 2016).

While it may be impossible to demonstrate entanglement for large objects at this time, scientists already believe that *many* distinct and separated entities, not just sub-atomic particles, may be able to become entangled or are entangled naturally. To date, the largest objects scientifically demonstrated to exhibit entanglement are millimeter-size diamond chips. But the thinking is that everything and everyone, being ultimately comprised of particles, may in theory have the potential for being or becoming entangled. Scientists are already, at least on paper, exploring the possibility of harnessing the power of entanglement, for example, for communication, which would then be instantaneous and un-hackable. Is it so unreasonable to consider that the prayers we say for a person we know and love may actually influence that person? Entanglement or connection may be the factor that might tip the scale of future studies of intercessory prayer into the realm of statistically significant improvement.

Again, let's be clear. I'm not suggesting here that your prayers will spontaneously heal or produce miraculous turnarounds in the lives of others. I believe that prayers for others, like prayers you say for your own benefit, simply direct God's bountiful energy in the direction of the prayer's focus.

As with all tenets of Cognitive Faith, prayer, as the only essential action of Cognitive Faith, should be grounded in reality, both in practice and expectation. While God's form and nature may be unknowable and divine, Cognitive Faith asserts that, in embracing God's existence, we can still embrace whatever evidence is eventually discovered, keep our minds open, and remain willing to explore current or evolving knowledge and truth.

Use Your Head – Politics in the Teens of the 21st Century

The late teens of the 21st century are interesting times, and I feel compelled to include some socio-political commentary based on current events. Though no politiphile, I consider myself to generally be a good citizen. I vote. I read about candidates and issues in our political forums. I know where I stand on most significant political topics, but allow that my views are subject to examination and revision. Over the years, I have at times disagreed with some of the political stances of our leadership, and at times felt deep pride and admiration. I have never, however, been so profoundly concerned about the leadership and administration of this country, and indeed the behavior of the entire political machine, as I am at this time. The issue I find most troubling is the continuing attack on truth and facts being adopted as a tactic.

I am well aware that politicians or other leaders have manipulated truth to achieve their ends, in all likelihood, since the dawn of human communication. I remember reading Shakespeare's *Julius Caesar* in high school and writing a paper on Marc Antony's artful verbal maneuvering to sway the people of Rome in the wake of the assassination of Caesar. "Friends, Romans, countrymen…" the speech famously starts, with Antony referring to Brutus as "an honorable man." Subtly but inexorably, Antony moves the people's opinion, ending with enflamed citizens who rebel against Brutus and the other murderers of Caesar. The crowd, so "with" Brutus during his speech, then so easily turned against him by Marc Anthony's.

In Kurt Anderson book, *Fantasyland: How America Went Haywire* (Random House, 2017), the author suggests that Americans in particular have a propensity for being swayed and for believing unlikely truths. Americans, he says, have in substantial population percentages fallen for countless false persuasive propositions since our earliest days. He cites many examples, from the 1600's Pilgrims' acceptance that they were venturing to a rich and wonderful new life, to the Witch Hunts in Salem in the 1700's, to the gold rush of the 1800's, to the 1900's eugenics movement, to pyramid financial schemes in the new millennium. While some far-fetched propositions may do little harm, say believing in ESP or the latest fad diet, for example, others, such as the Witch Hunts and subsequent trials, the subjugation of less desirable people associated with the eugenics movement, or the massive fraud we saw in financial institutions at the turn of the century and beyond, may have dangerous or even ruinous impact.

Whether Americans are or are not particularly susceptible, current political events do put the United States into the limelight on questions of truth and gullibility. We are seeing public statements coming from the highest political office that dismiss clearly verified facts, repeatedly calling them fake or fiction, and presenting certifiable untruths as facts. In 2017 the United States President personally used the communication forum of "tweeting" daily, often presenting opinions or stances on serious political subjects and according to CNN used the term "fake" over 400 times. Fact-checkers have delighted in identifying the countless inaccuracies in the President's regrettably unscripted error-ridden speeches and discourses. We are not dealing here with an occasional verbal misstep. We are dealing with dangerous vilifying or disrespectful characterization of ethnic groups, opposition members or dissenters. In epically nonsensical circular reasoning, we are told that if our leader believes or disbelieves something, that belief or disbelief, however erroneous or insupportable, is certified by his belief. More alarmingly, millions of Americans are accepting the flawed propositions.

Apply Critical Thinking

As part of the Critical Thinking course I designed for business mentioned earlier, we suggest a process for making rational, higher quality assessments of information.

When an issue, opinion or argument is presented, we suggest you first decide or assess the *apparent* veracity or credibility of the presented information. In this first pass, if we determine the initial information to be well supported and reliable, then we can proceed to the step of making a decision, accepting the information or taking action as the situation warrants. If however the presented information is from an unproven or questionable source or no support is provided, then we must determine if the issue or information is worth spending one's time or energy investigating. In some cases the issue is not important or of little consequence and therefore not worth spending time or energy investigating, and we can again proceed to the step of making a decision, accepting the information or taking action as the situation warrants. In this case we should acknowledge and understand that we *may* be accepting or basing our action on a flawed foundation. We do not know because we have not applied our best, higher thinking powers to the evaluate the information. If, however, the possible consequences are high or the issue is important, then here is where we are encouraged to exert that energy to investigate the issue. We might find that the information is supported, or not. In either case we now know if the information is flawed or sound, and we can take action based on that more informed foundation. A final question is whether special consideration should be given to the situation. (see Fig 6)

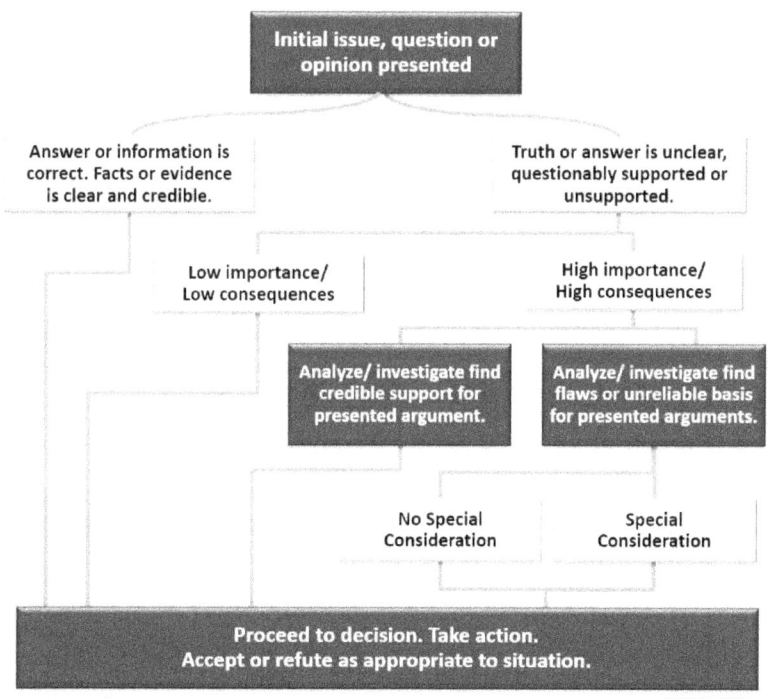

Fig. 6

Cognitive Faith

When teaching this course, I point out that flaws in logic and in support for arguments is common. We do not have to point out every flaw. Sometimes the more prudent decision is to know and understand the flaw but not act upon it. People who feel compelled to argue every little discrepancy in the reasoning of those around them can be seen as tiresome and pompous. The most elevated thinkers are capable of employing the highest level of critical thinking *and* making wise choices in the use of their knowledge. The overriding factor must be *the importance of the issues* and preferred objective of knowing and supporting the voracity in matters of significance for our lives and for our society.

For example, in 2017 and 2018 during the writing of this book, flames have been stoked to heighten a belief that American policies and liberal politics have failed our lower classes. While this is certainly not a new lament, current leadership seems to be pandering to a purportedly downtrodden *white* underclass, implying or in some cases saying outright, that employment and opportunities have been denied or usurped from them by liberal policies. The current administration promises their policy reforms will fix "the broken system." While undoubtedly reforms are in order in numerous areas of our government, too many people are just taking in the rhetoric, the tweets and the sound bites and forgetting to reflect on the veracity of the statements. We must ask if the assertions are meaningfully supported with reliable facts. The idea that significant improvements in prosperity can be bestowed upon a deserving but forgotten, or underrepresented, American population though a few simple policy adjustments seems questionable. And we must start with the question of whether the suggested desperate need for improvement is based in reality? Or is it pandering?

The economy in 2018 is and has been doing well for numerous years since the recession, in fact since 2010. Inflation is modest, unemployment is at the lowest rate in over 20 years, interest rates remain low, and the stock market has been doing well, overall, since the start of the recovery in 2010. By economic standards, the US is in good shape.

Furthermore, most Americans enjoy lifestyles and a level of prosperity *never before seen* in history. Even our lower economic classes have access to amenities and resources unheard of in truly disadvantaged countries. As a child in the sixties and seventies, living in a lower-*middle class* family, I wore second-hand clothes. Today many lower-class kids wear brand label clothes and shoes and carry smartphones, though perhaps purchased in discount stores. Still, such luxury was unthinkable in my youth. This is not to say that we are without social issues or disadvantaged people living in dire circumstances. We absolutely do have areas of deep poverty which we can and should be supporting, but is this the population for whom the promises of reform are being made?

Still, a substantial number of Americans *are* embracing the concept of [white] American disadvantage.

The rhetoric supposes that immigrants are taking Americans' jobs, global trade partners are taking advantage of America, undermining our manufacturing and causing jobs to migrate out of America. We seem to be casting about looking for a target, a bad guy to blame for these Americans not being able to buy a new Ford truck, or Converse shoes for their kids. Or, worse, looking for targets from whom this affluence or those opportunities may be wrested from because *they* are categorized as *not* entitled. Dangerous talk indeed.

Despite the comparative prosperity we now have, life satisfaction in the US overall is no longer even among the top ten countries (Organization for Economic Cooperation and Development, www.OECD.org, 2016). Complacency, feelings of further entitlement, and paradoxically, restless discontent, all contribute to an alarming level of unreasonableness and acceptance of flawed propositions. I think of Marc Antony and the fickle crowd, turned murderous. I also reflect on the German people in the late twenties and thirties listening to divisive, racist rhetoric of their leaders, while tapping into nationalistic sentiments.

I understand that average people, in allocating their non-working hours, must make choices about what stories and issues they can meaningfully research, and that they look to our leaders and our media to present digests of the truth. But what do we do when our leader is blatantly abusing the truth and subverting many of our most admirable principles. And when our media, our cherished free press, is so beleaguered that they seem resigned to highlighting the abundant absurdities, rather than providing careful reporting of the important doctrines being quietly undermined. Even thoughtful Americans, attempting to gain some perspective on current events, can become inured by the constant histrionics in the media, and recently there have been many.

I think of Anderson's assertion in Fantasyland, that Americans are already predisposed to reasoning failures. I think of a population in our country watching the current political events like they are part of a game show or a sit-com. Perhaps they find the provocative rhetoric enlivening. These Americans, who may have historically found politics boring and unconnected to their lives, are unfortunately, embarrassingly engaged by the current political antics, the wilder the better. But this spectacle and seemingly amusing dysfunction in our political system belies the seriousness of the issues, the unsettling dissolution of principles and the precedents being established.

But the concern here, the issue, is that we need to think. To use our reason, to apply higher, deeper thinking to the serious issues before us. I read somewhere that only a small portion of our population completes reading even one book over a year. Certainly reading deeply and conducting thoughtful research on issues is superseded for many in our current society by sound bites, tweets and episodes of television programming.

It is in this environment that I have been writing *Cognitive Faith*. In fact, this section did not even exist until later in the writing of the book as political events unfolded over the past couple of years. While I have been reflecting on and writing about science and God and rational faith, I have become keenly aware that a heretofore silent population has stepped forward and asserted its power; a population with little desire to engage in rational thought, about God, religion or any other issue. Furthermore, currently some extreme outliers are feeling empowered in their intransigence and immoderate beliefs. It is currently admissible, from the highest office in the country down to the lowliest radical factions to espouse divisive and prejudiced perspectives, or worse, to simply dub any opponent's presentation of facts or arguments to be fake or immaterial.

 I have tried while writing to remember that there are *smart, reasonable people* in our country, and to remember that the mental gullibility and extremism I lament above is exhibited only by segments of the American people. I also know that some of the concern I am presenting is not *religious* in nature. Still many of the central issues *are* clearly tied to so-called "moral" conservatism and belief systems that are often tied to religious doctrines. For example, gay rights, abortion rights, religious xenophobia.

 I know there are plenty of smart people who are devout Christians, and smart people of other religious affiliations, unlikely to go far down paths of extremism or intolerance. But I also feel it is prudent to recognize in today's world, that even very smart people, reasonable people, can find themselves backed into corners. If one is, however loosely, aligned with Christian or traditional, morally conservative beliefs, and extreme factions are currently pushing to roll back more moderate policies, particularly as related to individual freedoms, lifestyle choices, and religious intolerance, these less extreme associates will face challenges in determining where to stand.

Originally, I wanted *Cognitive Faith* to explore how faith, or belief in God, can be reconciled with rational thought and with our current and future scientific body of knowledge. I also hoped to show that faith can potentially help people improve their life. A crucial underlying prerequisite of Cognitive Faith is that we *keep our minds engaged*. My departure from traditional religion stemmed from my desire to look at and embrace facts, and rationally account for them, and still derive the benefits that faith can give. In Cognitive Faith, conscious choice, action and belief leads to empowerment. And, so empowered, we can use that strength to be a positive force in the world, aka to embrace goodness.

In the section on evil we explored why people might go along with odious societal dictates. In Germany during WWII it seems likely that while some embraced the Nazi dogma, certainly many more accepted the clearly racist ideology and subsequent murderous activities out of a desire to conform or perhaps out of self-interest or self-preservation. Though we cannot help but judge the general population of wartime Germany as ignoble here we Americans are today weighing our leader's and our government's declarations and decisions around internment, deportation and marginalization both of some of our own people and of the peoples of other cultures. This may be an extreme comparison. Still, I think of a frog placed in cool water and the heat then being raised.

    I am not suggesting that we disregard reasonable evaluation of our immigration policies. Nor reasonable evaluation of other foreign policies or trade agreements. But I am suggesting that we must resist and stand against racist, xenophobic, and discriminatory denial of individual freedoms, whether based on a specific interest group or a religion's agenda. We must keep our minds engaged and, if we embrace faith at all, pray for rational and considerate faith.

Closing

The book is called *Cognitive Faith* to highlight the human capacity to have faith and still keep our minds engaged. To encourage people to use their minds – you might say, use their God-given minds. The mental capabilities that set man apart from other animals are the very essence of what has brought us to this evolutionary point. We humans must continue to use our unique and powerful frontal-lobe capacities. The world has challenges yet to be addressed, societal problems, global problems. We need people to stay engaged, question current assumptions, and use the highest cognitive capabilities of their minds.

When people default to rote acceptance of beliefs or doctrines, or fail to critically assess the positions of their leaders, religious or political, intellectual discourse may be forfeited and unsupported facts or clear untruths can hobble the growth of knowledge and inquisitiveness. It should be obvious that science does not have all the answers to the whats, whys, and hows of the world and the universe, but we should not use that fact as permission to discount or dismiss all that we do know. We simply must not allow ourselves to be convinced of contrary nonsense just because it is presented as someone's opinion: our church's or our leaders'. As Daniel Patrick Moynihan is famously quoted as saying, "You are welcome to your own opinions but not to your own facts."

Of course, today we see a wide assortment of issues hindering intelligent discourse. Divisive political agendas, scams, and superficial and inane media content seem to be growing in prevalence. When people are caught up in lies, cons, or unprincipled or puerile content, the higher cognitive capabilities of critical thinking can be compromised or dulled. If fictitious or "I believe" positions are somehow accepted as truth, and people choose not to assess the underlying assumptions or facts, we see a lowering of the evolutionary intelligence bar, in some cases to alarming levels. It is easy to just accept what is presented or to go along with those around you. Thinking, assessing, finding and considering the facts or alternatives about assertions or what we are told is hard work. Especially when we are lulled into complacency by the comfort of being in a society that provides for all your needs, even if it comes on borrowed credit.

Closing

I worry about attitudes of entitlement, discontent, victimization, and dependence. This disinclination to engage higher cognitive functions is not, of course, the fault of religion or of flagging faith. Though I have lamented traditional religion's tendency to advance fantastical stories and flawed behavioral tenets, while unapologetically asking adherents to unquestioningly accept them, I nevertheless know that there are some very smart people in the rank and file of the religiously devout. Zealots aside, many perfectly rational and efficacious people quietly believe in their respective faiths. Whether "of two minds" or otherwise managing ambiguity or dissonance, they are able, quite successfully, thank you, to perform roles large or small in business, government, and even in the sciences, without issue. To these people, I apologize if my own rhetoric offends. If I allow that science does not have perfect answers to all life's questions and is nevertheless of extreme value, I can also allow that various religions may also be flawed and still have great value.

I believe in having faith. I hoped that, in writing *Cognitive Faith,* I might encourage people with no current faith or belief in God to explore the concept and potential benefits of having faith, without sacrificing their intellect. As I wrote, I came to embrace a further hope that readers currently affiliated with traditional religion might consider how the underlying tenets of their religion could influence their political and social stances, even if their personal views might be somewhat less dogmatic. The religiously devout might be encouraged to resist reflexive alignment with divisive stances.

Ultimately, this book became two intermingled books. One is an intellectual exploration of the concepts around science, religion, and faith. If you are completely secure and set in your spiritual beliefs, whether devoutly religious or devoutly atheist, I hope you at least found the book interesting. The expository purpose of the book *Cognitive Faith* was meant to encourage examination of the rational possibilities and perhaps limitations of faith and to compel you *to think* about faith. If you choose ultimately to discard any belief in God, do so thoughtfully. If you choose to steadfastly maintain belief in a traditional religion, do that thoughtfully as well.

The other purpose of the book is to provide an actionable path to the possible personal empowerment that can be tapped through faith. Now again, if your life is all good, and you are as successful, as fulfilled, and as healthy as you desire, perhaps this aspect of the *Cognitive Faith* book has little to offer you.

This book is not, however, meant to convert anyone. Cognitive Faith is not for people who need faith. There may be people in this world who lack spiritual grounding, struggle with unhappiness, dysfunction, and failures, and seem adrift. There are surely people who seem morally compromised. Yes, perhaps they might benefit from adopting Cognitive Faith, or, frankly, any supportive moral faith. But I feel there are many people who, like me, may have problems with self-limiting behaviors that constrain their ability to fully pursue happiness or life success. Or people with psychological, emotional, or physical challenges. Or even people who, less acutely, simply desire to elevate their personal, professional, or social success using the spiritual empowerment that is potentially available through Cognitive Faith. The simple actions suggested for the practice of Cognitive Faith may be worthwhile for these readers.

My faith has transformed my life. Though not a hillbilly, I related to many themes in Vance's book. There was a point in my life where I was at a crossroad. I took the path toward recovery, toward a productive and happy life. I believe this change was supported by the power of God, and would have been unlikely, if not impossible, for me without God's power. I tapped into that power and have kept the momentum going, adding more recovery, more productivity, and more success to my life through faith and prayer. I am not famous. I am not rich. I am, however, living a productive life. I am fully and responsibly self-supporting. I am socially accountable. I love and feel loved. And I can honestly say that I am happy.

In the introduction to this book, I stated that my hope was to offer some insights into my own unique view of faith. And to question and suggest alternatives to some of the propositions about faith, religion, and God commonly presented. The key actionable message of *Cognitive Faith* is that any person can adopt and tap into the power of faith.

Cognitive Faith

You need not even call it faith. You can call it meditation or affirmations. God doesn't care how you reach out, nor about the words or titles. The action of prayer begins the process of movement and an ensuing reaction. Just remember: no promises of miracles! But if a small miracle happens, I would not mind hearing about it. I promise you this: pray and take the next logical step toward the outcome you desire, and continue doing so, and you will be surprised at where your life goes.

www.ingramcontent.com/pod-product-compliance
Lightning Source LLC
Chambersburg PA
CBHW050554300426
44112CB00013B/1912